CAREERS
FOR
ANIMAL LOVERS
& Other Zoological Types

Louise Miller

Foreword by
Michael Robinson
Director
National Zoological Park

Printed on recyclable paper

 VGM Career Horizons
a division of *NTC Publishing Group*
Lincolnwood, Illinois USA

Library of Congress Cataloging-in-Publication Data

Miller, Louise, 1940–
    Careers for animal lovers & other zoological types / Louise Miller.

        p. cm. — (VGM careers for you series)
    Includes bibliographical references.
        1. Animal specialists—Vocational guidance. 2. Animal culture—Vocational
    guidance. I. Title. II. Title: Careers for animal lovers and other zoological types.
    III. Series.
    SF80.M55   1991
    636'.0023—dc20   90-50725
                                                                                            CIP

1995 Printing

Published by VGM Career Horizons, a division of NTC Publishing Group.
© 1991 by NTC Publishing Group, 4255 West Touhy Avenue,
Lincolnwood (Chicago), Illinois 60646-1975 U.S.A.
Manufactured in the United States of America.

    5 6 7 8 9 VP 9 8 7 6 5

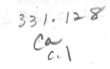
Dedication

To the late Susie and Eloise, Natty and Mugwump, and to the bouncingly alive Baby and Buster—this book is lovingly dedicated.

Contents

About the Author

Louise Miller has been an animal lover since she was first introduced to the delight of dogs with Sugar and to the charm of cats with Susie. The love goes on even for animals she does not know, domesticated or wild. In addition to animals, Miller also loves languages, especially English and German. She started out as a German teacher and teaches it today, after having studied in Vienna, Austria, and Bonn, Germany. She taught German at the Universities of Kansas, Missouri, and Illinois.

Her love of English led her to teaching, writing, editing, and proofreading the language. She has taught English at community and business colleges, has conducted writing workshops, and has worked both full time and free-lance for publishing houses. These include New Horizons Publishers, Compton's Encyclopedia, Rand McNally & Company, Richard D. Irwin, American Library Association, National Institute of Real Estate Brokers, and World Book. Miller was also research coordinator for television quiz shows in Los Angeles and has written a regular wildlife column for the Woodstock (Illinois) *Sentinel.*

Acknowledgments

Sara A. Meghrouni

Outreach Coordinator
Save the Dolphins Project
Earth Island Institute

Edythe B. Ledbetter

Defenders of Wildlife

Cindy Dominique

U.S. Dept. of the Interior
Fish and Wildlife Service

Virginia Van Sickle

Louisiana Dept. of Wildlife
and Fisheries

Vernon Bevill

State of Mississippi
Dept. of Wildlife, Fisheries
and Parks

Debra MacKenzie

New Jersey Division of Fish,
Game and Wildlife

Pete Squibb

State of Michigan
Dept. of Natural Resources

Arizona Game and Fish Dept.

Ron Byrns

Arkansas Game and Fish
Commission

State of California
Dept. of Fish and Game

Marlene Creech	North Carolina Wildlife Resources Commission
Vincent D. Yannone	Montana Dept. of Fish, Wildlife & Parks
Sue Wickham	State of Minnesota Dept. of Natural Resources
Arthur M. Johnson	New York State Dept. of Environmental Conservation
Jeff Smoller	State of Wisconsin Dept. of Natural Resources
Douglas R. Hansen	South Dakota Dept. of Game, Fish & Parks Division of Wildlife
J. Kenneth Terry	Ohio Dept. of Natural Resources
Elaine Weinberg	The Fire Plug Pet Store
George Ney	Cat House Originals
Patti Moran	National Association of Pet Sitters
Wendell C. Morse, DVM	International Association of Pet Cemeteries
Kay Alport	Dog & Cat Portraiture, Chicago
Allen C. Feldman	New Jersey Aquarium
John Caruso	The Anti-Cruelty Society Chicago
Donna Solomon	Animal Medical Center Chicago
Guy R. Hodge	The Humane Society of the United States
Carole C. Wilbourn	New York City
Jim Morgan	Morgan's Dogs, Chicago
Kenneth J. Shapiro	Psychologists for the Ethical Treatment of Animals

Foreword

Animals are marvels, but many species are in danger. A serious word about that first. I have no doubt that the fate of myriad species of life on earth is going to be the most pressing issue facing humankind in what remains of this century and for a substantial part of next century. This is because our burgeoning population—one that has tripled since the beginning of the century—is threatening the tropical rainforests that are the richest and most diverse natural areas left to us. Rainforest destruction has increased, according to one source, by 90 percent in the ten years from 1979 to 1989. As the countries of the so-called Third World struggle to achieve the standards of living that we enjoy, they "mine" the forests for timber and clear the trees to produce agricultural land on which to grow subsistence foods, cash crops, and eventually cattle. The very processes of agriculture and animal husbandry that made civilization possible now threaten the great tropical ecosystems. Burning the rainforests also adds to the greenhouse effect that may change the world's climate and result in global warming.

What does this have to do with careers with animals? It's really quite simple. If we are to keep a habitable planet, all of us have to be or to become biologically literate, understanding life's processes and the complex web of earth's ecology. I think this puts zoos, aquariums, botanic gardens, and natural history museums on the frontline of global environmental and conservation education. The basic attraction of living animals can be the key to understanding them. We can hasten informal education if we have inspiring, enthusiastic, and dedicated professionals. There are great careers in biological institutions that can help you to spend your life dedicated to one of the great causes of this century and the next. Working with animals means that life is literally in your hands.

Working with animals is a means of finding an outlet for idealism. It is also fundamentally worthwhile. You can educate and help save species from sure extinction. From panthers to pandas, we can help to breed those that are endangered. It can be both high technology and tender loving care. But it can also be fun and immensely satisfying. You can also prevent suffering, heal the sick, and save the distressed. There is magic in working with living animals—with all creatures great and small, common and rare, friendly and dangerous, exotic and native, young and old.

Ever since I was a very small boy, I have gloried in the living world around me, fascinated for a lifetime by pets and wildlife alike. It is a magical moment for me every time my cat Scuby taps me on the nose at night to signal that she wants to get under the sheets because it is too cold for her outside the bed. Pets help people to have calm and relaxed lives, and a career with domestic animals can be as rewarding as being a zoo director.

For me, animals from tropical fishes to tropical spiders have been both a stimulation and a joy. The sight of a newborn tiger or a newly hatched octopus is a ray of light in an often dull existence. If you feel this way about the marvels of biology, a career with animals is the place for you. This book can help you find it. Like all good things, it will mean hard work, but the rewards are beyond measure.

Michael H. Robinson
Director
National Zoological Park
Washington, D.C.

CHAPTER ONE

Exploring the Possibilities

*I*t may be true that loving animals is not a disease, but there are clear and definite symptoms of the condition. They may manifest themselves when you are very young, or they may come on in middle age or later. Animal lovers are not necessarily born that way—many potential animal lovers need exposure to the objects of their affection for their true feelings to be expressed. How do you know whether you are an animal lover, and if you are, how might that affect your career choices?

Since there is such a wide variety of careers in animal work, you might guess that there is also a wide variety of people who can fill those career slots. You would be right. From the veterinarian to the kennel attendant, from the shelter administrator to the records clerk, there is a job for you if you are committed at some level to the care, protection, healing, or general welfare of animals, or if you want to educate others in these areas.

The Making of an Animal Lover

Where do animal lovers come from? From your own backyard. The animal lover may have been the girl who always brought home a stray dog or cat for "just one meal" and kept the homeless waif for twenty years. Or he might have been the boy who would rather take nature walks or hike through the woods than go to the movies. Maybe the animal lover was the high school student who loved biology, zoology, or chemistry courses or who always went to cat or dog shows on weekends—or maybe the girl whose room was filled with stuffed animals because she couldn't have a real pet.

Other people live a longer time before they realize that they are animal lovers. It may strike them when, at 30 years old, they get their first pet dog, cat, bird, or fish. Or maybe a friend persuaded them to go birdwatching one weekend and they find themselves birdwatching every day from then on. Or they may realize that people in their neighborhood come to them when their pets are sick or injured. Still others spend their leisure time training the neighbors' dogs, even though they make their living as insurance salespeople, stockbrokers, or truck drivers.

Is Working with Animals Really for You?

If you have any of these symptoms or fit into any of these categories, you may be suited to a career in animal work. If you are still not sure, you might ask yourself these questions:

1. Do I genuinely care about the welfare of animals?

2. Am I willing to work long hours doing stressful work?

3. Can I live on a modest income?

4. Am I willing to go through years of education and/or training?

5. Do I like to work with people?

6. Do I have physical and mental strength and energy?

7. Can I exercise good judgment and solve problems under difficult circumstances?

8. Am I reliable, sensitive, compassionate, and empathetic?

9. Do I have good organizational and communication skills?

10. Am I willing to relocate to areas where jobs are available?

If you were able to answer "yes" to all of these questions, you are ready to explore the many careers available in animal work.

Types of Careers in Animal Work

The next step is to choose the type of work that best suits you and to be honest with yourself about your philosophy regarding the care and treatment of animals. You will also have to decide whether you want to work in the private or public sector and how much time you are willing to devote to training and education.

Some jobs will allow you to work directly with animals and make important decisions about their health and welfare, life and death. Others will require you to enforce laws regarding their safety, or to keep records on their vital statistics, or to see to it that they behave well or are properly nourished.

You may decide that your talents lie in painting, photographing, or writing about animals. You could decide to exhibit those works in your own gallery or magazine. Or you may create a whole new category of career based on your own particular talents and the animal needs you identify. You have a wide range of choices to explore.

Veterinarian

When most people think of a medical caretaker, they think of the local "vet." Whenever the family dog or cat gets sick or needs altering or spaying, the person we call to make things better is the veterinarian. Veterinarians in private practice are in every community to help protect the health and well-being of pets and to educate the owners on proper pet care and nutrition.

Veterinarians are also found in zoos and aquariums, in the classroom, in research laboratories, in regulatory agencies, in public health facilities, in the armed forces, in scientific agencies, and in wildlife management. They can also practice in humane shelters, at racetracks, on fur ranches, and at circuses. Some write pet advice columns for newspapers or magazines, conduct informational television shows, or prepare videotapes on the care or training of animals.

Veterinary Technician

Working alongside the veterinarian is the veterinary technician (commonly known as a *vet tech*). These animal workers are licensed and can prepare animals for surgery and administer anesthetics under the supervision of the veterinarian. These technicians often have degrees in biology or zoology and are the most highly skilled assistants to the veterinarian.

Animal Attendant

Animal, or kennel, attendants maintain the animals on an everyday basis by feeding and watering them, cleaning their cages or stalls, and washing their food dishes. They also watch for changes in behavior as possible symptoms of disease. They exercise the animals and check their environment for safety.

Therapist

Other caretakers work with the animal's personality problems in order to correct behavioral disorders, such as temperament, incompatability with other animals, and destructive tendencies. They generally work in private practice or clinics, but because this is a fairly new field, they may routinely be employed at shelters, zoos, aquariums, and racetracks in the future.

Protective Agencies

Many animal lovers go into animal work to provide shelter, to protest abuse, to educate the public about the needs and rights of animals, and to help protect endangered species. Protective agencies deal with both domesticated animals and wildlife, in cities and in rural areas. Protective agencies employ both paid administrative and clerical staff and also rely heavily on volunteers.

Trainer

Trainers of both domesticated and wild animals have the skills to teach animals to obey their commands. They are employed by pet owners, by the police or military, by movie and television producers, guide dog services, zoos, circuses, aquariums, and racetracks.

Groomer

Groomers often are also kennel operators and pet suppliers. Some also board and train animals. They usually confine their businesses to dogs, although some groom cats, too. Grooming service includes clipping nails, cleaning ears and teeth, bathing, clipping and trimming, and brushing and combing. Supplies sold at groomers' shops include collars, flea products, food, brushes, and combs.

Pet Sales and Service

If you want to specialize in selling pet products, you will have to love pets, including dogs, cats, fish, and birds, and should enjoy dealing with and advising pet owners. Store owners know something about pet behavior, nutritional needs, play needs, and habitat.

Zoos

Many career opportunities exist in zoos, including zoo director, curator, veterinarian, veterinary technician, and zoologist. Zoos also employ curators of exhibits, research, and education. Many zoos also have business managers and staff for the public relations department and gift shop, in addition to clerical workers.

Aquariums

Aquariums are generally headed by a director and often an assistant director. Most will also employ a general curator and specific curators for different collections. Veterinarians may be on the staff or be on call as needed. Aquariums also hire aquarists (aquarium zoologists) and librarians.

Creative Careers

Creative career possibilities in animal work range from pet and wildlife artist to writer, designer, and photographer. Illustrators are needed to prepare exhibits, charts, teaching aids, textbook designs, magazines, and educational programs. Photographers show their own work or sell to magazines and book publishers. Other artists specialize in pet portraits or paintings of wildlife.

Writers are employed by magazines and book publishers. They may write for children, adults, or specialists. Other creative people build cat condominiums or elaborate dog houses.

Pet Sitters and Pet Walkers

Pet sitting is a fast-growing industry because so many people own pets and because many two-income families are taken away from the home more often on business trips. You can be a pet sitter full-time or part-time. You will be expected to take care of dogs, cats, birds, and fish, as well as ferrets, rabbits, hamsters, gerbils, and snakes. Many pet sitters also water plants, walk the dogs, bring in the mail, and make security checks on the homes of the people who are away.

Pet Transporter

Some pet shop owners or kennel operators have branched out into the pet transport industry. This usually includes taxi service to and from the airport, but could include trips to the veterinarian or other health-related trips. The airport pickup and delivery service is especially helpful when the owner must arrive home after the pet. Transporters will often provide a boarding service for the pet until the owner arrives home.

Ornithologist

Bird lovers can find careers in research, education, and administration. Professional ornithologists work in universities and colleges, in state or federal agencies, in museums, and for conservation and consulting organizations.

Conservation and Wildlife Management

Both state and federal agencies employ workers in wildlife research, biology, habitat management, and population monitoring and management, or as fish and game wardens and interpreters. Private associations and not-for-profit agencies dealing with wildlife employ directors, legal counsel, corporate planning officers, financial officers, training directors, fundraisers, and membership and publications directors.

U.S. Department of the Interior

Jobs with the federal government are often scarce, but opportunities exist for biological science professionals and wildlife refuge managers. Others can work in interpretive or educational programs or as a special wildlife agent to investigate and enforce fish and wildlife laws.

Various administrative, clerical, and secretarial positions are available through the Fish and Wildlife Service, as well as openings for special program workers. Some fishing and wildlife technicians are also employed as well as equipment operators and craftspeople and maintenance technicians.

Animal-Related Businesses

In addition to being a pet shop owner, breeder, product salesperson, or feed supplier, which we are all familiar with, other opportunities for businesses related to animals exist and offer seemingly endless possibilities. They range from leading safaris in Africa to selling gourmet foods to "yuppy" puppies, from running pet insurance companies to pet cemeteries, from practicing cat astrology to tattoo registry, from renting guard dogs to jog with clients in the park to providing retired racing animals to private owners. According to your business experience or inclination, market needs, and changes in popular tastes, you can fairly well invent, contrive, combine, and create a new career track. Only your imagination (and perhaps a few local ordinances!) will limit you in your pursuit of the perfect career.

Responsibilities and Qualifications

Since there is such a wide range of possibilities in animal-related careers, qualifications, salaries, benefits, and responsibilities vary according to the job. Some jobs with animals are strictly administrative, such as the director of a shelter, and will be involved only in the broadest, most educational way with animal caretaking. On the other hand, veterinarians, technicians, attendants, and trainers work directly with the animals. Some careers require a high degree of education and training while others require very little or no previous experience in the field.

How to Get Further Training and Experience

It is always a good idea for anyone considering animal work—whatever your age, education, or experience—to volunteer or work part-time at a shelter, horse farm, boarding kennel, or wildlife facility before you make your final decision. Or you may want to work on a farm, ranch, or in a stable during your summer break from school or on your vacation—just to get a feel for the job.

Many facilities will be glad to open their doors to you for guided tours, informational interviews, or videotape presentations on careers in their field. Or they may have publications, such as pamphlets or brochures, for distribution to the public. Public libraries and bookstores also have specialized books, pamphlets, and videotapes available to you for study. These include the *Encyclopedia of Associations* and the *Occupational Outlook Handbook*. Your reference librarian will point you in the right direction.

Magazines specializing in cats, dogs, fish, birds, and wildlife can be found at public libraries, bookstores, and newsstands. Some specialize in care and training; others, in painting or photography of animals.

Dog trainers, kennel operators, and breeders may hire part-time help during their busy seasons. You should apply for these jobs to see if you are really suited to a lifetime career in the field.

Your local telephone directory and professional organizations will provide you with names and addresses of people to contact for specific information on education, training, and general qualifications required for their individual area of expertise. Advertisements in animal-related publications supply names and addresses of schools and training facilities that will help you launch your career. You should make sure that the facility at which you get your training is accredited or approved by the national professional association in your field.

Now it's up to you. You started out with the basic symptoms of loving animals and now it's time to do something about it. To make sure of the direction you're heading into, let's take a look at some more specific questions about your attitudes that will help you make up your mind about a possible career with animals.

1. I definitely want to work directly with animals.

2. I am willing to devote several more years to my education so that I can become a highly skilled professional.

3. I prefer to work with:
   a) cats and dogs
   b) horses, fish, or birds
   c) wild animals
   d) farm animals

4. I prefer a steady office job with standard benefits.

5. I want to help enforce the laws concerning animal welfare.

6. I do my best work when I'm managing other people and seeing that things run smoothly.

7. I am really good at typing, filing, answering telephone calls, and dealing with the public.

8. I have always been able to make animals listen to me and do what I tell them.

9. I have a very good business head and have entrepreneurial inclinations.

10. I want to write about animals with other creative people, such as artists, designers, photographers, and illustrators.

If you've answered "yes" to many of these questions, and if any of the possibilities mentioned in this chapter intrigue you, you're ready to go further in your exploration of careers in animal work. There is, truly, something for everyone—if they have the right symptoms!

CHAPTER TWO

Medical Caretakers
Frontline Healers

A nyone who has ever had a pet has gotten to know a vet. When Fido was sick, or Priscilla needed shots, or Spot needed to be spayed, we loaded our terrified friend into the car for a trip to the local animal hospital. Maybe even then we thought about becoming a veterinarian because we thought it would be a good thing to heal and comfort our companion animals.

Veterinarians

If we had looked into what it takes to become a veterinarian and what veterinarians actually do, we might have been surprised. We probably knew that the veterinarian knew how to diagnose and treat sick and injured animals, but we may not have known just how much education was required to earn a doctor of veterinary medicine (DVM) degree.

Education for Becoming a Veterinarian

Currently in the United States, a DVM can be earned in fewer than thirty accredited colleges. Just to qualify for admission to a school of veterinary medicine, you must have taken at least three years of "prevet" courses and have a college degree. You should also have a solid background in social sciences, language skills, mathematics, humanities, chemistry, biology, and physics. However, since each of the accredited veterinary colleges has different admission requirements, you should check the school of your choice and take the undergraduate courses required for that particular program.

As a student of veterinary medicine, you will initially be taking anatomy, physiology, pathology, pharmacology, and microbiology. At this stage, your education is mostly theoretical, although there also will be some laboratory work.

Later your work will be involved more with clinical and surgical training, working with animals and their owners. As might be expected, the emphasis in this stage will be on applied anatomy, diseases, obstetrics, and radiology. Public health, preventive medicine, and nutrition are dealt with at this point in your education, as well as professional ethics and business practices.

After all these hours of study and years of training, the veterinary graduate must still get a state license before going into practice. Veterinarians also must keep up with every new scientific discovery and technological advance throughout their careers.

Career Paths for Veterinarians

The great majority of veterinarians (about seventy-five percent) in this country work in private practice, and most of them work only on small animals, usually cats and dogs. A much smaller number work with larger animals, such as horses or farm animals; some work with both pets and livestock. All told, veterinarians look after the health of literally millions of animals per year.

Of the veterinarians who do not go into private practice, some become researchers or teachers. Others may find a career with a state or federal agency as regulatory agents, inspectors, disease control specialists, animal control workers, epidemiologists, or environmental workers.

Veterinarians who choose to educate the next generation of veterinarians are also encouraged to publish articles in professional journals and are involved in helping practicing veterinarians continue their education by teaching new techniques and methods.

Veterinarians who specialize in research can be found not only at the university, but also in private industry and government agencies. These veterinarians seek new ways to prevent health problems in animals, and in the process sometimes discover new ways to treat humans, too.

Veterinarians who choose to go into regulatory work are charged with the responsibility of controlling livestock diseases and making sure that those diseases do not affect the public. Those who work for the U.S. Department of Agriculture or state or local government agencies also have to inspect and sometimes quarantine animals that are brought into the country or across state lines.

Veterinarians in public health work for federal, state, or local governments, which affords them a wide variety of positions. As epidemiologists, they investigate outbreaks of diseases. Others work in the larger realm of the environment where they check water supplies or food processing plants for safety. They could also study the impact of pesticides and pollutants on the environment. In the laboratory, veterinarians work on immunization and quarantine programs.

As a veterinarian in the military services, you would probably be in the U.S. Army Veterinary Corps, a branch of the Army Medical Department. Under the umbrella of biomedical research and development, Army veterinarians are engaged in laboratory animal medicine, pathology, food hygiene, and preventive medicine, as well as providing regular veterinary services to Army animals.

The private sector employs veterinarians in research and development in such fields as pharmacology, parasitology, microbiology, and endocrinology, primarily for new product development. Some veterinarians work their way up to positions in production and quality control, marketing, sales, or even management. Companies in the food industry, agribusiness, and pharmaceuticals also are possibilities for employment.

Basically, wherever animals are, there also are veterinarians— in neighborhood animal hospitals, in shelters, in zoos and aquariums, at racetracks, and in wildlife management facilities. No matter where they work, veterinarians must like and respect animals and also be able to work well with people, very often under stressful circumstances.

Making a Living as a Veterinarian

According to your choice of veterinary work, your working conditions will vary. In private practice, universities, laboratories, and offices, you will generally work regular hours with a steady income and good benefits. However, if you work with livestock or horses, you may be working outdoors in all kinds of weather. Hours can be long and irregular and the work can be hazardous.

Although veterinarians' incomes also vary according to background, experience, and specialization, as a new graduate you can expect to start at about $15,000–$25,000 per year after graduation. As you gain experience, your salary in government, private industry, colleges, or the military can reach from $35,000 to $65,000 per year.

The future prospects for employment as a veterinarian seem to be quite good, especially for those with training in specialties such as toxicology, environmental or space medicine, and disease control.

Veterinary Technician

Working alongside the veterinarian is the veterinary technician, a comparatively new position in animal care. Because of increased demands on the veterinarian, more and more animals are receiving the specialized training of the technician. Although duties may vary from practice to practice, the primary responsibilities of a veterinary technician usually include recording information about patients, preparing patients and equipment for surgery, collecting specimens, performing specific laboratory and first-aid procedures, treating wounds, and dealing with patients' owners. All of this work is done under the direct supervision of the veterinarian, scientist, or senior technician.

Education for Becoming a Veterinary Technician

You can begin preparing for a career in veterinary technology early. Most veterinary technician programs require a high school diploma or its equivalent and often successful completion of specific courses in high school for admission. Therefore, you may want to talk to your career counselor for help in finding the admission requirements for the programs that suit you best. Most will require a rather strong background in science in either high school or college.

The next step in becoming a veterinary technician is to attend one of the programs of the forty-eight fully accredited colleges of veterinary technology. Required coursework will usually include chemistry, mathematics, humanities, communication skills, and biology. In addition, more specialized coursework will be offered, such as ethics, physiology, anatomy, biochemistry, nutrition, and parasitology. At the end of two years of study, you will receive an associate in applied science or similar degree. Many accredited schools suggest that you use the summer break for obtaining practical job-related experience at a clinic or shelter.

After you receive your degree as a veterinary technician, you may have to become registered or certified by the state in which you will practice. Registration requirements vary from state to state. The American Veterinary Medical Association provides a synopsis of these regulations and the American Association of Laboratory Animal Science handles examination and registration procedures for veterinary technicians specializing in laboratory animals.

Once you are on the job, in addition to the required technical skills, you will need a large dose of patience, empathy, and understanding as you treat sick and injured animals and deal with their owners, who are also under stress. The scope of your responsibilities will depend on the veterinarian for whom you work and the type of facility where you work. These facilities include clinics, shelters, zoos, horse farms, racetracks, kennels, laboratories, and even meat-packing facilities. In laboratories you may be expected to feed and care for the animals, maintain the equipment, inspect the carcasses, and keep records.

Making a Living as a Veterinary Technician

Currently, the annual starting salary for degreed technicians is from about $10,000 to $16,000 per year. More experienced graduates' salaries range from about $12,000 to $24,000 per year. Depending on where you work, benefits might include social security, health insurance, paid vacation, and retirement programs. Your promotions within the field will be based largely on performance, attitude, anticipation of veterinarians' needs, and initiative.

Professional associations make it possible for veterinary technicians to continue their education and to network with others in the field, either at social events or in a professional setting. The national professional organization in this field is the North American Veterinary Technician Association, but the American Veterinary Medical Association also provides lists of local and state organizations for veterinary technicians.

Animal Care Attendant

If you have a real commitment to the everyday care, feeding, and cleaning of animals, you may choose to become a full- or part-time animal care attendant. Grooming and exercising animals are included in this job, as well as cleaning cages. These duties are performed in animal shelters and hospitals, kennels, stables, grooming shops, zoos, and aquariums. You might even work with an ambulance crew or as an overnight shelter attendant. You may be called on to keep basic records and, in some cases, to do some manual labor, such as basic carpentry, painting, lawn maintenance, or digging graves for deceased animals.

If you are looking for a glamour job in animal work, this one is probably not for you. As an attendant, your work involves hard, often dirty, often repetitious, but absolutely necessary work. Working closely with the animals, you will get to know their personalities, temperaments, and needs firsthand. Your rewards are largely intangible, but you will have the joy of experiencing the positive responses of a recovering or lonely animal as it is emotionally or physically healing from injury or disease.

Jobs for Animal Care Attendants

Working as an animal care attendant in a stable means that you would be responsible for cleaning out the barns or stalls, feeding the horses, brushing them, and trimming their manes and tails. Then you may have to harness and saddle the horses, rub them down, exercise them, and cool them down.

Horse attendants also clean the tack room and polish the saddles. Feed bags and other supplies for the stable may be heavy, but you may be called on to unload them when they are delivered.

In a shelter, either private or public, your responsibilities as an animal care attendant would be different from those in the stable. Basic cleaning, grooming, and feeding are the same. At a shelter, however, you may also keep records and screen potential adopters. Sometimes shelter attendants also serve as animal control officers who pick up stray animals and rescue animals who are trapped or otherwise impaired. Attendants may also field calls concerning potential abuse or cruelty toward animals. Many shelters now use attendants as adoption counselors to people who have never owned a pet. Since the attendants know the adoptive pets so well, they are able to match them up with their new owners.

In a veterinary hospital or clinic, animal care attendants perform the basic daily duties for the well-being of the animals. In addition, they may help prepare equipment and instruments for surgery or help hold the animals while they are being treated by the veterinarian. All instructions given by the veterinarian regarding diet and care of the sick or injured animal have to be followed precisely by the animal care attendant. The attendant in a hospital may also be called on to communicate with the pets' owners and perform some clerical duties, such as answering telephones, keeping records, and making appointments.

If you work as an attendant in a laboratory, you may have to keep records on experiments, observe effects of drugs or medication on the animals, assist in the preparation of special diets or nutritional needs of the animals, and take care of recovering animals.

You should keep in mind that some of the animals in your care may die, and for someone who has cared for an animal, death can be a traumatic experience. Before becoming an animal care attendant, you should think about whether you can deal with the reality of pain and death of animals you love.

Becoming an Animal Care Attendant

Since there are no educational or training requirements for the animal care attendant, many people come to this job as volunteers and work up to a staff position. As a volunteer, you will get the opportunity to see whether you have what it takes to be an attendant. You should also think about which area of caretaking you would feel most comfortable in—the hospital, shelter, stable, laboratory, or aquarium.

If you are still in school and are contemplating working as an attendant, you should take English, mathematics, and social studies. Additionally, biology, chemistry, science, physiology, or psychology would be helpful. Any courses in animal behavior and business administration are a bonus.

There is a rather high turnover rate among animal care attendants so employment opportunities are good. Also, people are demanding better care of their animals. Salaries, however, are generally poor. The work is steady, though, because animals often need round-the-clock attention and you cannot always leave work at five P.M. Benefits usually include paid vacation, health and life insurance, a pension plan, and sick days.

If you are already working but are thinking about changing your career to animal work, you might want to work as a volunteer at an animal hospital, kennel, shelter, or training facility. Remember that your physical strength, emotional sensitivity, ability to deal with difficult situations, patience, and thoroughness are valuable qualities to bring to any work with animals. They are especially valuable, however, for those whose jobs require daily physical contact with pets, livestock, or wildlife.

Pet Therapist

A fairly new career opportunity for animal caretakers is that of pet therapist or psychologist. At present, there are no specific qualifications or educational paths that are required, but as the field grows, standards will be imposed and professional organizations will probably be founded. For now, however, it could be called an open field for career possibilities. Although therapists usually specialize in companion animals, there will probably be room for therapists in wildlife management and farm animals as more is learned about animal behavior.

One of the earliest pioneers in the field of pet therapy is Carole Wilbourn who operates out of a veterinary center in New York City. She specializes in feline behavioral disorders, devising total therapeutic programs for emotionally based problems that may lead to physiological disorders. Carole also writes a monthly column for *Cat Fancy* magazine called "Cats on the Couch" and has written several books on the subject. She has appeared on radio and on regional and network television shows, and conducts classes on cat behavior. She makes house calls, too.

Carole majored in psychology in college and went on to work with various organizations and individuals with cat problems. She then founded a veterinary hospital that dealt exclusively with cats.

Like humans, cats can become chronically anxious because of stress. This emotional problem can eventually lead to physiological illness. Cat therapists should be familiar with feline anatomy and behavioral patterns and messages. They should also be sensitive to both animal and owner in determining what therapeutic course to take.

Cats experience stress, grief, happiness, and sadness, and may express these emotions in antisocial behavior, damage to property, or not using the litter pan. Part of the therapy may be accompanied by tapes of "New Age" music. Played back later at home, these tapes can help the cat recapture peaceful feelings experienced in therapy.

Cats are currently considered the most popular companion animal, partially because they are more self-sufficient than dogs. They are perfect pets for working people, apartment dwellers, and single people. As the number of cat owners continues to grow, so probably will the need for pet therapists.

You must have a genuine concern and sensitivity for animals if you want to enter this field. A background in psychology or animal behavior would be extremely helpful. As the field expands, training in animal husbandry, wildlife management, and biology may also be required.

The pioneer work being done by pet therapists now may also serve as the basis for further research and treatment for farm and other animals. Your imagination and creativity in this new field may come into play, as well as your technical skills and empathy and compassion.

Animal Caretakers Are Important to Everyone

You might ask yourself why there is such a wide range of work available for those who choose to be animal caretakers. From the most highly skilled professional—the veterinarian—to the kennel attendant, animal caretakers play a vital role in the life of our society. Healthy, loving companion animals bring a great deal of joy to their human owners and provide lifelong companionship. They have been known to help sick people get better and older people feel young again. Having a pet in your life is a privilege and offers all of us a daily glimpse into the life and behavior of another species.

Companion animals are becoming more popular with people who live in small city apartments, and no longer belong only to suburban families with backyards or wide open spaces. With the demands and dangers of city life and with more owners working outside the home for longer hours, the pet may need special psychological help to cope with the anxieties associated with new experiences.

Animals in zoos and aquariums also need proper nutrition, a compatible habitat, and proper medical attention. The same applies to wild animals. Since the natural habitats of these animals have been destroyed in many parts of the world, one of the main functions of zoos, aquariums, and wildlife management facilities is to provide the animals with the kind of environment and food that is conducive to their health and well-being, as well as their propagation.

Captive wild animals provide humans with a look at species that would otherwise not be available, which should lead to understanding and respect for other species. Because of the size of these facilities and of the animals themselves, many caretakers are needed for their welfare—veterinarians, attendants, technicians, nutritionists, and biologists.

Colleges and universities specializing in veterinary medicine rely on other veterinarians to teach, publish, consult, and perform research. An ability to transmit ideas and to evaluate progress of the students is needed in this career, in addition to a thorough knowledge of veterinary medicine. Without the teachers to guide the next generation of caretakers, whole generations of animals might be lost due to injury, neglect, disease, and overpopulation.

Without veterinarians in regulatory work, diseases could spread rapidly from animals to humans, especially if the animals have come into the country from other parts of the world. So the veterinarian in regulatory work is very much concerned with the health and well-being of humans, if only indirectly.

Of course, diseases are more often transmitted from animal to animal, and that's why animal epidemiologists are important. Tracing the origin of the disease and finding a cure will help preserve the species involved, as well as the lives of the afflicted animals.

Pollution affects both humans and animals in many ways every day. Our water supply and air quality are crucial to sustain all forms of life, as well as to ensure future generations. Pesticides affect the food chain for all land creatures, and sea animals are just as affected by oil spills as we are. Veterinarians who specialize in environmental hazards for animals will again indirectly aid human preservation.

Animals used for sport, such as race horses, need excellent daily care and nutrition if they are to perform to their full potential. Many caretakers are necessary to maintain these sleek animals' well-being. And when they take off from the starting gate, it's easy to see why they are so cherished.

Animal caretakers, then, are necessary to preserve the health of individual animals as well as that of the species. Indirectly, they also help to preserve the welfare of humans by helping to preserve the vital ecological balance between and among the many species on the planet.

Where Do Animal Caretakers Work?

Once you have decided that you want to become part of that link between healthy and cared-for animals and the people who rely on them for beauty, pleasure, joy, and companionship, you will want to take a look at the possible places where you might be employed in your new career.

Here is where you can work as a veterinarian:

in private practice

in hospitals and clinics

in zoological parks

in aquariums

in private and public shelters

for regulatory agencies

at racetracks

for environmental organizations

in wildlife management facilities

at universities and colleges

in laboratories

in the military service

in food-processing plants

at pharmaceutical companies

at horse farms and stables

in kennels

Here is where you can work as a veterinary technician:

in private practice

in hospitals and clinics

in zoological parks

in aquariums

in private and public shelters

at racetracks

in wildlife management facilities

in the military service

at horse farms and stables

in kennels

Here is where you can work as an animal attendant:

in hospitals and clinics

in zoological parks

in aquariums

in private and public shelters

in wildlife management facilities

in laboratories

in the military service

in horse farms and stables

in kennels

Here is where you can work as a pet therapist:

in private practice

in owners' homes

in hospitals and clinics

in classrooms

on a magazine staff

in a shelter

The Next Step

Now you know which caretaker careers are available and how to prepare for them. You also know why these careers are so important to the physical and emotional welfare of animals, and indirectly, of humans. And you now know a little bit about where you would be working as a caretaker.

The next step is to do a little more research to be sure that you're on the right track. Volunteer at your local shelter or clinic. Contact your local animal hospital and see if a veterinarian or veterinary technician would talk to you about their job. Or maybe you could work part time as an animal attendant. You can read every article there is on pet therapy or specialized books from your community library. Don't be afraid to plunge in and ask, read, and research. There is a lot of work to be done and caretakers are usually willing to talk about their work. They are, after all, hard-working professionals who are proud of their work and want to share their information with interested people. And remember—the sooner you start, the sooner you'll be working with the animals you love!

CHAPTER THREE

Protective Agencies
Shelters and Refuges

U ntil people are educated in the humane treatment of animals, there will be a need for animal rescue teams, rehabilitation services, and shelters. Many organizations are trying hard to get the word out to school children and adults about the way to live with our animal friends. Still, companion animals, wild animals, and livestock are often abused, mistreated, and abandoned by those who should be taking care of them. Outdoor animals are often injured by natural predators, traps, and motorized vehicles. Birds often fly into buildings or power lines. Other animals are victims of oil spills, environmental pollution, or land development that seriously damages or destroys their natural habitat.

However animals arrive at the point of needing help, they can find medical care, rehabilitation, and a temporary home. If it is a domesticated animal, private and public shelters are available. Wildlife refuges and rehabilitation centers either provide a natural habitat for undomesticated animals or care for them until they are released back into the wild.

Working at a Private Animal Shelter

Private shelters for domesticated animals usually house dogs and cats, but often other animals, such as pigs, chickens, and birds, are brought in. These shelters are generally not-for-profit agencies and are organized like a business. Therefore, they provide careers for administrative and clerical workers, investigators, lawyers, and accountants. Secretaries and receptionists are often employed at shelters, as well as records clerks and computer operators. These positions are all in addition to veterinarians, veterinary technicians, and animal care attendants.

Shelters in large cities can take in thousands of animals a year. Most shelters never turn an animal away for any reason. This is because most private shelters are founded on a specific philosophy regarding the care and treatment of animals. Some, for instance, keep animals in cages; others do not. Some will euthanize an animal (kill it painlessly and humanely) after a certain period of time; others will only euthanize when the veterinarian decrees that the animal cannot be saved or is destined to suffer if kept alive. Some take in only cats or dogs; others take in any animal. If you decide to work in a shelter, you should check their guiding philosophy regarding the treatment of animals before you apply.

Since so many animals are brought to shelters every year (some may average around 20,000), the shelter has to be well organized on many different levels, which allows for a variety of career opportunities and responsibilities.

Administrator

In a typical shelter, administrators might include an executive director and an administrative director. Many shelters have a volunteer board of directors to whom the administrative heads report.

The executive director is the overall administrator for the organization and operation of all departments and programs in the shelter. These departments may include humane education, shelter management, fundraising, public relations, the clinic, and field service. As spokesperson for the shelter, the executive director may be called on to be interviewed for local radio and television shows or newspapers, to give testimony at public hearings, or to speak at community gatherings.

The administrative director may work more directly with fundraising programs and membership recruitment and may also be in charge of personnel and selected programs. For either job, an education, such as a bachelor's degree, or experience in business administration is extremely helpful. As in any business, the administrator must be adept in communication skills, both written and oral; capable of working well with people; and well organized in order to see to the smooth operation of the shelter.

As the administrator of a shelter, you should also have training or experience in animal shelter management. You may become executive director as a result of a promotion from within the shelter, or you may be brought in from the outside if you are an exceptionally qualified candidate, such as a veterinarian with experience in operating an animal clinic or hospital. A commercial kennel manager may also qualify for the executive director position.

Shelter Manager

Many private shelters also have a shelter manager who oversees the daily operation of the kennels, hires and supervises kennel staff, and establishes and maintains procedures for the kennels. A liberal arts education would help a person to become a shelter manager, but an animal care attendant could also be promoted into the position. If you are currently an animal care attendant, it would be a good idea to take night courses or attend workshops in animal science, business administration, management, or related topics in order to be considered for promotion to shelter manager since supervisory skills are required for this job.

Shelter managers usually report directly to the executive director and may have at least one assistant manager reporting to them. Together, the shelter manager and assistant manager supervise receiving agents and kennel attendants. Receiving agents are those employees who take the animals in and, if necessary, perform euthanasia. In some shelters, the animal care attendants also serve as adoption counselors. In this role they screen and interview applicants for part of the day and take care of the animals for the rest of the day.

An assistant shelter manager could be promoted to shelter manager, especially if he or she had some background in veterinary technology, animal science, kennel management, or animal husbandry. Salary will vary according to location and facility. (As we've already learned, no one should go into animal work who is aspiring to be a millionaire!)

Humane Investigator

Most shelters employ humane investigators (sometimes called agents or cruelty investigators) who pick up stray animals; rescue injured or trapped animals; or investigate reports of animal abuse, negligence, or abandonment. These agents can issue citations or warnings to offenders and even assist in the prosecution of offenders. Humane investigators generally need a high school education, but specialized programs are not offered at most colleges at the undergraduate level. However, if you are interested in becoming a humane investigator, you might study animal science or veterinary technology, in addition to courses in criminology or law enforcement. Some states require certification, although you may also be able to serve as an apprentice under a more experienced investigator and receive sufficient training for this position.

In small or rural communities, humane investigators may be employed only on a part-time basis. Salaries will vary accordingly. However, promotions are possible for humane investigators, generally to some kind of supervisory investigative position, or to the positions of assistant shelter manager or shelter manager.

Humane Educator

Many shelters believe so strongly in educating the public, especially children, in the humane treatment of animals that "humane educator" has become a specialized title in humane animal work. The humane education department of a private shelter upholds and implements the philosophy of the individual agency, which, as has been mentioned, may differ between agencies. Mainly, though, humane educators stress kindness and compassion to all living beings.

Most shelters send their educators out into the grade schools of their communities to teach children about values, attitudes, pet care, and animal awareness. Working with students in all grades of one school over a period of three to five days, the educator covers many topics, such as animal needs and rights, dangers to animals, overpopulation problems and solutions, and the general responsibilities of pet owners. In the upper grades, the students are told about the work of a humane society and careers in humane work. Usually tours of the shelter can also be arranged. More than twenty states consider humane education so important that they have enacted laws for compulsory classroom humane education.

In addition to making these presentations, humane educators also provide teachers and students with informational handouts and packets. Some shelters, depending on their size and budget, produce periodic newsletters, videos, and tapes for school use.

Larger shelters located in larger cities generally have humane education departments, to which the humane educator belongs. The department is headed by a director who coordinates all humane education programs, including those involving schools, libraries, museums, and other shelters. The director also deals with personnel problems and usually reports directly to the executive director or administrative director.

If you are considering a career as a humane educator, you should have a college degree in education or a related field. A minor in animal science is helpful, as well as courses in journalism, outdoor recreation, public relations, or environmental education. To become director of a humane education department, you may need a master's degree in education. At this level, courses in management, writing, and public speaking would be desirable. The Humane Society of the United States offers regional workshops in this field through the National Association for the Advancement of Humane Education.

As a humane educator, your salary will vary with the size of the facility and community. Generally, the larger shelters within the larger cities will be able to offer the highest salaries, as well as more opportunities for jobs and promotions.

A Humane Education Manager

An overwhelming love of animals as a child is not necessarily a criterion for later work with animals. You don't even have to spend all your time taking nature walks or hiking through the woods. Because of the structure of the shelter, all kinds of talents and qualities are needed.

John Caruso, current manager of the Humane Education Department of The Anti-Cruelty Society in Chicago, majored in English and philosophy in college, not animal husbandry or biology. He says he was not one of those children who brought home stray cats and dogs. But he feels strongly that a thorough liberal arts background is valuable for anyone in humane education because it can help people analyze situations and solve problems—abilities that are needed in a management position.

John also had some background in public speaking and theater. So when he applied for a job in customer service at the shelter, they thought he was better suited to education. He was an educator under three separate managers, each of whom had a distinctive approach to the job. When the manager position became available, he applied, and, because of his on-the-job training, became manager.

John is a nontypical animal lover. Because he is a manager, he does not have direct contact with animals, and thus has no need for scientific training. And even though a bachelor's or master's degree in education is preferable for this position, his strong liberal arts education, public speaking experience, and on-the-job training qualified him for this position.

Humane educators often begin at the shelter as volunteers or kennel attendants, because many shelters have a policy of promoting from within. This promotion policy is a strong drawing point for employees and often compensates for generally low pay. John believes that, in addition, most shelters offer good benefits packages and sometimes tuition reimbursement programs for those who wish to continue their education.

Humane educators at The Anti-Cruelty Society give presentations to more than 40,000 students annually. In addition, they generate all kinds of written material and often handle more than 200 calls on pet behavior per month. They are currently writing a book and have assisted in the production of a film for fifth- and sixth-graders called *Protecting the Web.*

In order to alleviate too much repetition in their school presentations, John and his staff try to vary their work, present different angles or perspectives, and come up with new ideas for presenting basic principles. And even though humane educators never really know whether the public understands and applies the knowledge they work so hard to present, most feel that the work is important enough for them to persevere. And even with the frustration of not getting immediate results, John feels fairly certain that what he and his staff are doing is effective and has helped people and animals live more harmoniously together.

Shelter Clinics

Private shelters also have clinics that are headed by a chief veterinarian, to whom other veterinarians and technicians report. The clinic may also use externs from a local college or university to work along with the professionals.

Veterinarians and technicians from a shelter often operate a traveling spay/neuter clinic for the whole community. One of the major tasks for veterinarians at a shelter is to spay and neuter, and they have to be prepared to handle a volume of work that a veterinarian in a private practice may not have.

Volunteer and Volunteer Coordinator

Most shelters, because they are not-for-profit organizations, depend on a dedicated group of volunteers on whom they can call for a variety of challenges, tasks, and responsibilities. These volunteers may eventually decide to make working with animals their career, as many do. In charge of training and assigning these volunteers is the volunteer coordinator. This position requires organizational as well as communication skills, plus an ability to work well with and supervise others.

Two jobs that volunteers might be involved in are working for a pet therapy program and manning the phones on a pet care hotline. The animal behaviorist on staff usually assists in training volunteers for these programs. Pet therapy programs bring volunteers and animals to hospitals and senior citizens' homes so that sick and infirm people get a temporary pet to cuddle. Sometimes emotionally disturbed children will be brought to the shelter for caring sessions with the animals. On a pet care hotline, volunteers counsel pet owners over the phone about the pet's behavior and training. Although these volunteers work closely with other professional staff people, they are assigned and scheduled by the coordinator.

Clerical Worker

No smoothly operating organization can function without efficient clerical workers. Secretaries are needed for the administrative staff, and a switchboard operator, file clerk, and computer operator are also part of most shelters. Since extensive records are kept on both the owners and the animals, the position of records clerk is a necessity in a shelter, unless the computer operator handles this function.

Those at the front desk are sometimes called customer service agents because they are the first contact the public has with the agency. They may also serve as switchboard operators and file clerks. In some shelters, they issue identification tags to the animals, record all pertinent data about an animal onto cards, and provide information about adoption procedures to the public.

The outlook for jobs for clerical workers in shelters is quite good, especially if you have a high school diploma and a basic knowledge of grammar, spelling, punctuation, and mathematics. Applicants for secretarial and typing positions should type at least 60 words per minute; secretaries may also be required to take shorthand at a minimum of 80 words per minute. Reliability, cooperation, punctuality, and organizational skills are looked upon favorably by potential employers.

Although all clerical positions do not require direct contact with animals, front desk personnel should be able to work well with people, who are sometimes upset over the loss of an animal, and with the animals that they may be checking in for adoption. In these cases, empathy and compassion can prove important qualities to have. Some clerical workers may be called on to do light typing or operate business machines, such as photocopiers, postage meters, calculators, and mail sorting machines.

Working at an Animal Control Agency

Animal control agencies, run by the city, county, state, or federal government, are structured roughly the same as private shelters. They employ administrators, clerical workers, veterinarians, technicians, animal care attendants, and animal control officers. The difference between a humane shelter and an animal control agency is in philosophy and intent.

Humane shelters have been established to prevent and/or lessen suffering and abuse of animals. The primary objective of the animal control agency, on the other hand, is to make sure that animals, especially strays, do not impinge on the lives of the residents of the community. The legal responsibilities of animal control agencies include patrolling for stray animals, impounding them according to local laws, and investigating residents' complaints about loud barking, injuries inflicted by animals, and property damage caused by pets or strays.

Director of Animal Control

The animal control agency is headed by the director of animal control who functions as the chief administrator, responsible for all agency programs and personnel. Job qualifications and education for this position would be generally the same as for the executive director of a humane shelter. Since the public agency is funded by the government, however, there is no real need for fundraising talents. Animal control directors, as government employees, must know and uphold the animal control laws of their individual communities.

Animal Control Officers

Animal control officers, also called animal control agents, are authorized to inspect pet shops, kennels, stables, and related businesses to see that the owners are complying with animal welfare regulations. If the community has laws about rabies or other inoculations, the animal control officer must enforce them. The animal control officer may be called on to rescue trapped animals, conduct obedience and pet care classes, enforce licensing laws, and investigate possible animal abuse cases. These officers should also know the rudiments of first aid, especially when dealing with trapped, abused, or injured animals.

Animal control officers may have to work with other government departments, such as the police or health departments; environmental, wildlife, or conservation agencies; and, on occasion, with private humane shelters.

As with humane investigators, their counterparts in private shelters, animal control officers are usually required to have a high school diploma. Any additional undergraduate courses you take to prepare for this job should include criminology and some animal science or veterinary technology training. You will receive further training when you are hired, usually from an experienced agent. This kind of work demands not only knowledge of local animal ordinances, but also an ability to make good judgments and to cope with the stress imposed by the field work.

When it becomes necessary for the animal control officer to bring in stray animals for impoundment, the strays are turned over to the shelter manager who keeps records of all animals in the kennels. Kennel attendants then see to the daily care, feeding, and cleaning of the animals, just as in a humane shelter. This is usually where euthanasia takes place, if that becomes necessary.

Animal Shelter or Animal Control?

Since many of the jobs in private and public shelters are somewhat equivalent in terms of responsibilities, education, and qualifications, your career decision will probably be based on your philosophy toward animals. Humane societies are opposed, for example, to euthanasia except when the animal, in the veterinarian's opinion, is terminally suffering or when the shelter is so overpopulated that euthanasia is the only solution. Humane shelters also do not believe in using impounded animals for laboratory experiments, hunting animals illegally or indiscriminately, using leghold traps, or raising animals in an artificial environment.

Government agencies, on the other hand, may not be bound by the same philosophy as humane shelters. So if you are pursuing a career in shelter work, you may want to investigate the purpose and operating principles of the shelters you are considering for employment. Since most medium- and large-sized cities have both a humane shelter (perhaps more than one) and an animal control agency, your career opportunities are better there than in smaller, rural communities.

Working in Wildlife Management

The smaller, rural communities will, however, afford you the opportunity to work in wildlife refuges and rehabilitation centers. Wildlife is, of course, defined as all animals that are not domesticated. Fish may be included in this definition, although they are sometimes put into a different category.

The entire field of wildlife management in this country is fairly new—about 50 years old. It is generally defined as the human maintenance and manipulation of natural resources to benefit the total environment. In that broad context, the saving of individual animals and the protection and preservation of entire species is vital. Wildlife and its preservation is important to the ecological balance of the planet. Efforts at maintaining this balance are becoming increasingly important in these times of greater and greater environmental pollution and increased habitat destruction.

Wildlife Refuges

Many positions in wildlife management are to be found in wildlife refuges. These refuges may be public or private, with most being run by either state, federal, or provincial (Canadian) governmental agencies. Wildlife refuges provide shelter for endangered species, protect those species that are threatened, and study habitat and diseases of wildlife. Careers in wildlife management at refuges often require arduous study and training, long hours, determination, and a deep commitment to protection and preservation to individual animals and whole species.

Refuges and rehabilitation centers must have an organizational structure if they are to run smoothly. Therefore, they need administrators and clerical workers, wildlife and research biologists, and often fishery biologists. Veterinarians and volunteer coordinators may round out the picture.

Refuge Manager

The U.S. Fish and Wildlife Service of the U.S. Department of the Interior runs hundreds of wildlife refuges across the country. Refuge managers' responsibilities are primarily to protect indigenous and migratory fish and wildlife and to control and regulate hunting and fishing at the refuges. The manager is a highly skilled professional who has probably come up through the ranks and who has a great deal of technical knowledge. However, as an administrator, the refuge manager also must have a good business sense, work well with people, and know how to stretch a budget dollar.

Managers should have a college degree, preferably in a physical or biological science. Specifically, they should have completed nine hours of zoology and six hours in wildlife courses. Managers should also have a mastery of English, including speaking, reading, and writing. Psychology, geography, public relations, and economics courses are also very helpful.

If you are still in high school and are thinking of wildlife management as a career, you should study math, English, chemistry, and biology. Any experience working on committees, conducting meetings, or writing for newspapers or yearbooks will also help you.

Since wildlife work is highly competitive, you are encouraged to get a master's degree or a doctorate in wildlife-related fields to increase your chances of employment. Many colleges and universities in North America now offer courses leading to a degree in wildlife management.

Wildlife Biologist

Wildlife biologists are also employed at refuges. Their work includes the study of wildlife distribution, habitat, ecology, mortality, and economic value. In addition, they conduct wildlife programs, apply results of research to wildlife management, work with the restoration or creation of wildlife habitats, and help to control diseases in wildlife.

Wildlife biologists working as research scientists have to be knowledgeable about wildlife population dynamics, land use, and environmental pollution. Their primary training must be in the scientific method of collecting, analyzing, and objectively reporting data to their supervisors and other refuges for future practical applications.

Fishery biologists work with aquatic organisms in fish hatcheries where rearing and stocking operations are performed. Habitat, history, and classification of these organisms are also part of the study of fishery biologists.

Wildlife biologists should have a college degree with at least 30 semester hours in biology. These would include nine hours in wildlife-related subjects, 12 hours in zoology, and nine hours in botany.

For more information on wildlife management, see chapter eight, "Wildlife Conservation and Management."

Working at a Rehabilitation Center

Animal rehabilitation centers, operated by private or public agencies, are devoted to the treatment of sick or injured wildlife. Many specialize in one species or one type of animal within a species. Rehabilitation centers are necessary because all forms of wildlife are subject to natural disasters as well as manmade hazards. Wildlife animals suffer during tornadoes, blizzards, earthquakes, and droughts. They are sickened by oil spills and water and air pollution. They are injured or wounded by traps, gunshot, collisions, live wires, and natural predators. And they are subject to disease, just as humans are.

Rehabilitation centers usually are headed by a professional manager and employ wildlife or fishery biologists and volunteer coordinators. Educational requirements are similar to those for positions in the refuge, but for those biologists who will work directly with injured animals, special emphasis may be placed on training or course work in clinical pathology, basic shock cycles, anatomy and physiology, drug dosage, physical therapy, and emergency care. Clinical pathology courses will include some laboratory procedures in blood work, parasitology, and urinalysis in wildlife animals. You will be taught how to draw blood, test white cell counts, and test for heartworm.

To work in a rehabilitation center, you will need to know how to treat wounds, heal fractures, and determine antibiotic treatments. If you work with birds, you must be able to clean and care for birds caught and injured in oil spills. Some tasks in a rehabilitation center are more complex, such as setting up a physical therapy program for a particular kind of animal or species. Some wildlife biologists working at rehabilitation centers exclusively perform research into ways of reducing exposure of wildlife to fatal diseases.

Volunteer coordinators can learn the specific skills they need to perform their jobs at workshops and seminars. Such courses might focus on recruiting, training, motivating, and delegating, as well as hiring and firing procedures and burnout management.

The Next Step

The International Wildlife Council is the professional organization to contact for further information in this field. Members include administrators, educators, researchers, veterinarians, and humane workers. Although it is not a licensing agency, it does offer certified course work in various aspects of animal rehabilitation.

If you choose to work for the U.S. Department of the Interior as a federal employee, you will have to get an application form from any Federal Job Information Center in most large cities. The Competition Notice (CN-0400) that comes with the application form will inform you of any restrictions regarding specialized positions and locations. Send your completed form to the Office of Personnel Management, Staffing Service Center Examining Office, P.O. Box 9025, Macon, GA 31297-4599.

Now you should have a better idea of the opportunities that are available in shelters, animal control agencies, refuges, and rehabilitation centers. If you are still interested in exploring these possibilities, you need to make a few basic decisions. They will revolve around whether you want to work for a public or private agency; how much time you want to devote to education and training; which kind of animal, domesticated or wild, you wish to care for every day; whether you want to be an administrator or a field worker; and what your philosophy is about the care and treatment of animals.

Whatever your choice, keep in mind that direct work with any animal in need of help can be stressful and even traumatic. Your physical and emotional strength, compassion, and technical skills will be necessary to see you through the long hours of difficult work. But you should also be aware that the rewards are equal to the difficulty. Your work is essential to the well being of all creatures—including humans.

CHAPTER FOUR

Trainers and Handlers

M aybe your particular strength and capabilities lie in another area—teaching an animal to behave, to perform certain tricks, to guard the house, or to provide guidance for handicapped people. Many people develop the rudiments of training skills with their first pet. For example, perhaps you were famous on your block for housebreaking your puppy in record time. Or you were able to make your dog heel or stop or jump on command.

Perhaps you lived in a rural area and grew up familiar with horses and how to handle them. Or you may have been fascinated by the lion tamer at the circus or Lassie in the movies. You may have even performed the miraculous—taught a cat to jump through a hoop!

If any of these descriptions fit you, there are opportunities awaiting you in the field of animal training. Again, you will have to decide which animals you prefer to deal with and which kind of training you would be best at. Then you can set your course accordingly.

Your natural talents and abilities must, of course, be honed into actual technical skills, which can be acquired in several ways. For some, college courses will be the key to successful employment in animal training. Others learn training skills in the military or law enforcement agencies. Still others start out as volunteers or apprentices to a professional trainer or work at shows to gain experience. Others have combined these methods and natural talents to create a career since no strict professional or educational standards have been established for trainers.

Dog Trainers and Handlers

Probably the greatest number of instructors in the field today are dog trainers. Because of the popularity of dogs as pets, trainers are called upon to teach them how to behave and follow owners' instructions. Training methods may vary, but generally the pet will learn not to chew up the furniture or articles of clothing, not to sleep on the furniture, or not to run into the street. They will also learn how to walk on a leash and to sit, stay, and lie down on command. Puppies also need to be housebroken.

Some trainers deal exclusively with the animal who is boarded at the training facility during the training period. Others conduct classes with owners and pets together. Some trainers work for larger training centers; others are self-employed. Some work as trainers full time; others, only part time. Those who are full-time, self-employed trainers may supply other services, such as boarding and selling food and training supplies. They may also provide counseling to people about to purchase a pet dog and give advice on nutrition for the pet.

Gaining Education and Experience as a Dog Trainer

It is possible to become a dog trainer by combining your basic aptitude with on-the-job training. If you feel that animal training is the career you want to pursue, you could begin as a part-time volunteer at a training facility. The facility could be a larger training academy or a smaller private business. Different kinds of facilities may have different qualifications for employment.

They may, for instance, require that you have previous experience with animals or animal-related education, or they may prefer to train you totally in their own methods. As an apprentice, you may be required to work for up to five years under the supervision of an experienced trainer. Since there are no professional standards or licensing procedures for animal trainers, you should exercise extreme caution in selecting a trainer to apprentice with. You should investigate their training methods and philosophy, including how and when they physically punish disobedient animals. Your professional reputation as a trainer may well hinge upon your choice of instructor.

Because of the lack of defined standards in the training field and the risk of choosing an incompetent instructor, more and more people who choose animal training are opting for some kind of college education related to the job. College course work might include psychology, animal behavior, animal science, or veterinary technology as a basis. This formal education will enhance your on-the-job training and put you in a better position for employment.

Attending dog training academies is yet another route to employment as a trainer. These courses are usually fairly short, however, with the trainee acting largely as a kennel attendant. There is usually just some very basic instruction in actual animal training. You should be wary of these academies because they are typically quite expensive and are usually not accredited.

Training Assist Dogs

As a dog trainer, your instruction is not limited to pet behavior problems. You may, for example, want to specialize in training seeing-eye dogs to help blind people lead more independent lives. There are only a few places in this country that train seeing-eye dogs, so the competition for job openings is fierce. In order to qualify for employment as a seeing-eye dog trainer, you must be physically strong and have previous work experience with animals. It is preferable to have an educational background in veterinary technology, animal science, or to have work experience in a kennel, hospital, or farm. No frivolous people need apply!

Most people are familiar with seeing-eye dogs, which are now quite common. But deaf people need help, too—in getting around, waking up on time, and knowing when the telephone or doorbell rings. Even such basic security devices as smoke detectors, sirens, and fire alarms are geared to people who can hear. Life can be dangerous and lonely for people who can't hear these sounds and whose freedom of movement is thus restricted.

Enter the dog who acts as its owner's ears! These dogs must be able to differentiate sounds and signal the owner appropriately, according to whether the sound is an alarm clock or smoke detector. They have to be alert and energetic, healthy and vigorous. Trainers of such dogs need both people and animal skills in order to match owner to dog and consider the individual personalities and needs of both.

Often assist dogs have been rescued from the pound. They usually go through training for more than a year with a hearing-impaired handler before handler and dog are able to work as a team. Assist Dogs International, a professional organization, can help you find the right training program for you and inform you of required qualifications.

Training Working Dogs

The U.S. Customs Service, the military, law enforcement, and other government agencies employ animal trainers and handlers to train animals, mainly dogs, for such tasks as detecting specific scents at border crossings or airport terminals, finding injured people trapped in wreckage caused by earthquakes or other disasters, and even attacking enemies. These agencies usually train their own personnel and thus often require no specialized education or training experience for employment. The dogs that are trained as guard dogs, either for law enforcement agencies or private owners, must have obedience training first. The best dogs for this type of training should be aggressive but obedient. Therefore, you would probably be working with such breeds as German shepherds, Doberman pinschers, or rottweilers.

These dogs usually begin training with the handler at the kennel at the age of three to four months. Then they are brought to the actual worksite to continue their training. Dogs who guard homes should be good barkers, since that is what usually deters burglars; however, they must be gentle and loving pets, too. But guard-dog trainers will train the dogs to bite and attack on command if their work calls for that type of action.

Handling Show Dogs

Dog handlers are also used to show animals at dog shows. They usually work with individual dogs. Aspiring show dog handlers must have several years of experience as owners and exhibitors of purebreds in order to qualify for apprenticeship with an experienced handler. As professional show handlers, they often show dogs for those who do not know how or are too busy to show their own animals.

Employment Outlook

The demand for qualified obedience instructors is good within the public and private sectors, even though there are so many unqualified people in the field. Since trainers need not be licensed or certified in most places, anyone can open up a shop in any neighborhood in this country. If you choose this field, then, you should find a qualified and reputable trainer to apprentice with, get thorough on-the-job training, take some job-related courses, and build up a good reputation in your community.

As an employee of a federal or local governmental agency, your salary will be set according to your job category, and you can count on a fair amount of job security. Self-employed trainers can set their own fees and hours, which generally tend to be long and irregular.

A Professional Dog Trainer

Jim Morgan, a professional dog trainer in a large midwestern city, opened up his own training facility in May 1989 after running his business from the back of a Chevette! He used to load up his little car with dogs of all sizes and bring them to the park to train. During this period, he was trying to build up a full-time business, based largely on a lot of natural talent and a real desire to turn talent into a livelihood. He was not sure that anyone could really earn a living training dogs, since he found training dogs so easy and had a hard time believing that anyone couldn't do it.

Jim thinks that the demand for professional obedience training for pets came about when women had to work outside the home. In the traditional family, Mom housebroke the family dog and taught it to sit, fetch, heel, and walk on a leash.

Now Jim and his wife and children live upstairs and the dogs they train and board live downstairs in what Jim considers to be the perfect arrangement—the dogs are never alone and he doesn't have to worry about them if they should get sick or need attention. He specializes in obedience training, but because of his customers' fears of break-ins and street crime, about 10 percent of his business is devoted to protection training.

Jim has evolved his own unique training methods and style. And since he is self-employed, he can set his own fees. Although he did not set out to be a trainer, Jim thinks that people in high school or college should consider taking biology, animal science, or any preveterinary courses to prepare for their career as a trainer. And he believes that anyone who wants to work with dogs has to go to dog shows, attend obedience training classes, work in kennels, read dog-related publications, and talk to everyone he or she can in the field. He would urge anyone who is considering this career to volunteer or work part-time caring for dogs, observing other trainers, and asking questions.

Be Careful about Getting Education

Jim is fully aware of the lack of professional standards in the field and warns anyone who wants to learn how to train dogs to be very careful about false claims and deceptive practices.

Dog-related publications carry advertisements for dog training academies and schools, but Jim thinks that if you decide to attend these courses, you should find out the names of recent graduates and whether they are presently working as trainers. In other words, since there are no accrediting standards for training facilities for dog trainers, you at least should find out if those who have completed the course are competent and employable. According to Jim, the National Association of Obedience Instructors is now working toward setting professional standards for accreditation and certification of licensed trainers and that this probably will be the norm for the future. People considering dog training as a career should keep up with this trend toward professionalization so that they can fulfill the requirements set forth in those standards.

If you are thinking about training dogs for a living, you also need to be aware that you will be dealing with human owners. That part of the job is the most difficult for Jim and is why he insists that the dog stay with him for a two-week training period—without the owner. During that time, the owner is only allowed to view the dog at a distance, for example, from the car while the dog is being trained in the park. Jim believes in training every dog individually and that rapport must be established with the animal before the actual commands are taught. With some dogs, Jim achieves almost instant rapport; other dogs catch on only at the last minute.

Jim prefers to train dogs when they are young while they still have nothing that needs to be unlearned. After the dog is trained, he offers weekly owners' classes to reinforce training or to teach the dogs new commands.

Jim has never had to advertise his services—satisfied customers let others know of his skill and pass it on by word of mouth to family, friends, and neighbors. He has trained thousands of dogs and suggests that to make a living in dog training, you must love dogs, love working with them, and be prepared to work long and hard. But in spite of the hard work, so far Jim wouldn't dream of having it any other way.

Horse Trainers

Those who choose to train horses take many of the same entry paths as dog trainers: apprenticeship under a professional trainer, educational background in animal science or technology, or experience as a volunteer or hobbyist. Once you have entered one of these paths, you need to determine where and what you want to train.

If you decide to come up through the ranks, you will be able to learn in farms, stables, or racetracks. On the other hand, a college education will train you in many of the skills you will need and give you some practical experience. It may also improve your existing skills.

You will have to decide on the kind of horse you feel most comfortable with—saddle horse, quarter horse, Lippizan, among others. You will then want to decide whether you want to train horses for steeplechase, dressage, racing, or show jumping. With any of these choices, you also should be able to work well with people—the riders who are also being trained and the owners of the horses.

All of these options require determination, endurance, patience, physical strength, and, of course, a love of horses. Horse training is different from dog training because the emphasis is not on behavior or protection, but rather on performing specific tasks for competition and prizes. Race horses, for example, long part of our cultural scene, require specialized training because the owner's prestige and often livelihood is at stake. Amateur equestrians depend on the horse's training for international competitions that may lead to professional standing. And all of these events and competitions depend on the competency of the trainer who will prepare the horse and rider for the specific purpose they are capable of and designate as their goal.

Something Different: A Cat Trainer

For most of us, dog and horse training seem familiar. We know that dogs and horses love to be trained to perform, protect, and compete. But what about cats? "Never!" you say.

But if you really want to train your cat to play a toy piano, roll over and play dead, sit up and beg, or jump through a hoop, you might want to contact George Ney in Wauconda, Illinois. George was hit hard by the oil crisis of the 1970s. When the housing industry foundered, his business as a tile and carpeting salesman also began to fall apart.

Being a creative person, however, George used some of that unused carpeting and started to build cat houses, including condos, duplexes, and ranch styles, as well as couches, chairs, lamps, and tables. In order to sell them, he brought them to cat shows where he became moderately successful and fairly well known for his imaginative designs.

Eventually, and instinctively, George had begun to try some basic tricks with one of his cats. Surprisingly, the cat learned to roll over, to beg, and to shake hands. When he told people about this performing cat, they all laughed in disbelief. Until they saw it for themselves! And soon more and more people were seeing it, too.

George began putting on volunteer demonstrations at local establishments and then bringing the act to cat shows, where he and the cat put on a show and sold some cat furniture, too. Eventually he taught the cat more and more tricks, such as sitting in a high chair, rolling a barrel, and "answering" a toy telephone. He added more cats and is now traveling most weekends with his feline troupe, logging about 40,000 miles a year. They have appeared in malls, convention halls, schools, nursing homes, on television, and in commercials. And they're still going strong.

How to Train Your Cat

George's training methods and style are based on love and fun. They include gentleness, pacing, and patience. George has learned that cats' attention spans are not long. Training sessions don't last more than ten minutes an hour, but are held as many times during the day as possible, between the first and last priority of any cat—naps. Working with natural feline abilities, such as jumping and rolling, as well as a love of petting, George devised ways to make cats respond to certain cues. He also learned to reduce the larger trick down into its simpler component parts.

Some of the problems with training cats often originate in humans' misunderstanding of cats. They are really not as aloof and independent as some think, but they certainly do not have the inclination toward training that dogs and horses do. George believes that you should start with a neutered cat who already knows how to use a litter pan. He suggests you start training a cat with simple tasks such as using a scratching post or staying off the furniture. Catnip and a water spray are usually enough to teach most cats what you require as acceptable behavior.

To learn tricks, your cat should be at least eight weeks old and enjoy being touched and petted. You need to pay attention and let the cat give you cues as to its fatigue, boredom, or lack of interest in any particular trick. Repetition, praise, and a training table to practice on are essential components in the training of cats.

If you are planning to make a living with your trained cats, you also have to be sure that your cats can travel well and can adapt to the changes of life on the road. Cats are usually very territorial, and can be very upset by changes in their environment, including noises. You might consider training more animals than you actually bring with you to any given show, so that they will have a resting period between trips.

Since there is no market for watch cats or any need for cats to protect home or property, training cats to perform should be considered a method of bonding between owner and cat and a source of pleasure for both.

George Ney, in his unique capacity, has decided to make a career of it. He literally created this career out of economic necessity and love, and thus had no previous formal training or education either in making cat furniture or training cats. But as a businessman, he needs to be concerned with publicity and promotion, booking and scheduling, travel and veterinarian expenses. Being affiliated with professional associations such as the American Cat Fanciers' Association, Canadian Cat Association, International Cat Association, and Cat Fanciers' Association is very helpful in such a career. Cat periodicals tell George when and where national shows are taking place and local papers and bulletins inform him of local events and organizations that may be sources of future business.

As with many other careers having to do with animals, definite educational and training criteria and standards need not be established in advance. Sometimes you just have to combine natural talent, economic necessity, hard work, and love of animals to create a career path that provides you with economic security, a real sense of satisfaction, pleasure, and fun. Ask George Ney. He did it.

Your Career as an Animal Trainer

You may decide to apply your training talents exclusively to the performing arts, such as movies, television commercials and shows, special events and performances, circuses, and carnivals. The animals you might train would include dogs, cats, horses, elephants, lions, and tigers. Often zoological parks or aquariums have performing animals as part of their exhibits, and trained animals may also appear at trade fairs and shows, parties, and community events.

You may work as an independent contractor who hires out to movie or television producers, zookeepers, aquarium curators, or show organizers to teach specialized tricks to specific animals. Or a particular animal may be used as the regular representative of a particular product or service in a continuing series of television commercials.

As an independent contractor, you may set your own per diem or per performance fee. Fees will vary according to whether you are performing at a children's party or for a commercial or movie. If one of your animals has a major role in a movie or is the star of a commercial series, your fee might be quite high. If you are employed by a particular institution on a regular basis, you will receive an annual salary with normal benefits.

Trainers may also decide to write books or articles or even put together audio- or videotapes on successful training techniques and unusual experiences. They also may combine their training skills with other services, such as counseling, nutritional advice, kennel operation, or pet product sales.

Some trainers may use their experience and skill as a stepping-stone to other positions within their field or to open up their own franchise operation or combination shop. As you gain experience and a solid reputation, you will begin to train the trainees or apprentices. And as professional organizations start up, you may become involved in their work.

These choices are basically up to you, according to your inclinations and capabilities. Decide which animal you are most comfortable with—dogs, cats, horses, wild animals. Do you want to train them for specific skills? Do you want to work for another person or be an independent contractor? Are you willing to be on call for the animals every day, all day? Would you like to have a combination business, such as trainer/kennel operator? Do you want to train guide dogs or police dogs?

The choices are there; you just need to make them. But there's one thing about yourself you should be sure of before you decide to become either a trainer or handler: you must love to work with animals!

CHAPTER FIVE

Animal-Related Businesses

There are other people besides veterinarians and shelter workers who take care of animals or see to the needs of owners. These include the business people who provide supplies and services that maintain the animals' health and well-being, take care of pets while owners are away, and even dispose of the pets' remains when they die. At all times between birth and death, animals have needs that must be met, and there is usually a career path associated with these needs.

We will discuss these basic needs of animals and how they can be served, and then branch out into more frivolous possibilities, including the creation of new careers based on changing needs and technological advances. Then you will be left to decide which possibility fits your own needs, education, inclinations, and talents. We will begin with the neighborhood pet store.

Neighborhood Pet Store

The pet store is where we find everything related to pets for sale—from cat litter and litter pans to toys, ID tags, and scratching posts; from catnip to cages, collars, and carriers; from food and flea powder to training supplies and shampoo. We also find items that are *not* for sale—such as advice, nutritional charts, pictures of other pets that have been brought in by customers, notices of lost and found animals, and referrals to veterinarians, breeders, trainers, and kennel operators. Over the phone you can receive prices, friendly counsel, and general, all-around caring conversation to comfort you in your concern for your pet's problem.

With all of this going on, there is barely room for proprietor or customer, but somehow you get what you need with maybe a discount coupon for your next purchase. With luck, this owner will never move out of the neighborhood or will at least be considerate enough to sell the business to someone just as caring.

A Pet-Store Owner

Such a store and such an owner is Elaine Weinberg who owns and operates The Fire Plug pet store. According to Elaine, a pet shop owner has a million stories to tell—stories that revolve around the idiosyncracies of both pets and their owners and the changes in taste and preference that have evolved over the past twenty-four years.

It was back then that Elaine, who was working for a plumbing contractor, and her sister decided to open up a pet store. They had saved up some money and had given themselves a one-year time limit to succeed or quit. Just to be on the safe side, Elaine kept her day job and worked for the store evenings and weekends.

Elaine and her sister had grown up in a family that considered it normal to have lots of kids and animals around. Her father even branded as selfish people who didn't have a pet. With that background, why *wouldn't* she and her sister open up a pet shop? Maybe because they had no retail store experience; maybe because they didn't know about procedures, policies, and laws governing such businesses.

But lack of practical knowledge never deterred them because they were willing to learn as they went along. They learned that few people had confidence in them for the long run; they learned that customers and pets dictated their business choices, no matter what they thought was right. They learned that they didn't want to stock bird and fish supplies because most of their customers were dog and cat owners. They learned that they did not believe in selling animals at their store. And they learned that they loved pet owners and their pets.

That may seem like a lot to learn—and it was. But when you've lived in a neighborhood for fifty years and you love animals, and you get to know their owners, and you're doing what you love, what's a little learning?

Elaine and her sister moved into a former hardware store 24 years ago and turned it into a pet store that has been there ever since. To hear Elaine tell about it is to relive a quarter-century of growth. If you visit Elaine's shop in Chicago, you will probably be shown her photos of pets that were customers over the years. Elaine feels attached to all of them.

Although she has a very small office space now, it is probably bigger than the deli booth across the street that she and her sister used as an office when they first started out. Elaine is living proof that you can work for animals, even in a peripheral way, without having training in the field. And that is because, in part, luxurious office space, personal ego, and accumulation of wealth were not important to her. Serving animals and helping their owners were of primary interest to her and her sister. They thought that it was possible to stock the store with supplies and then sell those supplies—a very simple system indeed. Many people, including suppliers, helped them to learn about laws, customs, and traditions of the retail business. So they persevered and the business has survived for nearly twenty-five years. And although the shop no longer sells bird and fish supplies, the loving owners of dogs and cats will keep Elaine in business for another twenty-five years.

Elaine now works with an assistant and deals with trusted suppliers. The one in New York delivers supplies every five weeks; the local supplier delivers every two weeks, except in an emergency when Elaine can get what she wants sooner. Even though Elaine had no retail experience, she learned early to watch trends in owners' tastes and determine which supplies she should stock.

She suggests that you will probably need three outside people to help get you started: an accountant, an attorney, and an insurance agent. You may also have to find a steady supplier that you can rely on and perhaps one or two assistants to help with inventory and sales.

Successful pet-shop owners listen to what owners say they need for their pets. Shop owners should also keep in touch with groomers, trainers, veterinarians, and breeders. Most will also want to attend shows, read trade publications, and keep up with trends in nutrition, play needs, and new products. Attending business seminars or classes is also very helpful. But the primary characteristic of a successful pet shop owner is a love of animals and an understanding of owners. Getting to know both pets and owners and accommodating your business to them should be your major concern.

Pet Grooming

A neighborhood business that involves much direct contact with animals is that of a pet groomer. Some groomers are also kennel operators and some also sell pet care products. A much smaller number also breed and train animals. Most groomers handle dogs only, while a small number groom cats. Usually groomers have to work full-time. The typical grooming shop has two to three employees, often family members.

According to a recent survey, the majority of groomers went into business because of their love of animals. But groomers also must enjoy working with people since groomers deal directly with pet owners. Groomers are needed in both small towns and big cities and can earn high salaries according to their location.

Groomers approach their career in one of three ways: by serving an apprenticeship under an experienced groomer, by attending a trade school, or by teaching themselves. Most participate in training programs throughout their careers and continue to read trade journals. Others may also attend seminars and classes. Some groomers who own their own shops may also provide ongoing training for their employees. They also may attend professional conventions and trade shows.

There are specific services that are provided at most grooming operations, which include nail clipping, cleaning ears and teeth, bathing, dipping, hot-oil treatments, brushing, combing, and clipping and trimming coats. The customer may opt for individual services or a complete grooming for a set fee. Nail clipping is often considered a separate service.

Products that groomers sell include collars, flea products, food, clothes, and beds. They may also sell grooming supplies, such as shampoo, brushes, and combs. If you decide to board animals in addition to providing grooming services, you will have to provide cages and runs. You should also plan on summer being your busiest season for boarding.

In addition to hiring other groomers, a shop owner may have a veterinarian on call, an accountant to handle the books, a lawyer, and an insurance agent. Most shop owners handle their own publicity, which may consist of just a display ad in the yellow pages of the local telephone directory. Word-of-mouth advertising is also very effective, with radio, television, direct mail, and billboards being other possibilities.

Groomers, as is the case with all people who choose to work directly with animals, often work long hours and occasionally suffer burnout. Grooming shop owners must sometimes be on call. They also must deal with a host of other problems to be solved and decisions to be made. For example, as an owner you might have trouble finding competent and reliable employees. You also need to carefully select a location that will be attractive to customers and find a shop where overhead is not too high.

Education and Employment Outlook

As with animal trainers, no real educational standards or licensing procedures for pet groomers are mandatory in most places. Therefore, if you choose to apprentice with an experienced groomer, be sure to check that groomer's credentials and reputation. The National Dog Groomers Association of America, Inc. is a professional organization that offers workshops and certification tests to all members. Through such organizations, members can network and attend conventions, seminars, and competitions.

As a shop owner, you will be able to set your own fees. You will probably be able to charge more if you are located in a prosperous neighborhood in a large city than if you are in a poorer neighborhood in a small town. Many groomers feel that the lack of professional status prevents them from charging fees that are commensurate with their work and skills. You may want to check fees that are prevalent in your area and charge accordingly.

Animals need grooming to maintain their appearance and good health. No matter what part of the country you live in, your services as a groomer will be vital and necessary to animals and their owners. There is a good future for you as a groomer. But before you commit yourself to this career, talk to groomers and volunteer at grooming facilities. That way, your final choice will be the right one.

A Cat House Architect

Healthy pets need an environment that both provides amusement and fulfills their basic needs. For example, cats have a real need to climb, jump, nap, scratch, play, and feel sheltered—and they like to do all that in a place they can call their own. Enter George Ney—again. We met him earlier as a cat trainer, but his imagination and love of cats led him into yet another line of work. George creates elaborate cat houses, condominiums, scratching posts, duplexes, castles, perches, and race cars—almost any kind of diggings that cats would love.

Each creation always has at least one tree limb incorporated into it, since trees are cats' natural scratching posts. Since George used to sell carpeting, he is able to use carpet overstock on the posts and perches.

Observing cats long enough will tell you that they love comfort, security, and heights. George capitalized on his knowledge of cats' needs and his knowledge of carpentry. Starting out simply with spools, he then built taller and more elaborate houses with different sizes and shapes of perches, platforms, and tubes. Most kittens will stay in the lower parts of a more elaborate house until they are big enough to climb or jump to the top. George's cat condos and other furniture were so attractive to cats and owners alike that he is now able to make his living selling them.

George's designs for the houses and furniture are limited only by his imagination. He combines tree limbs, tubing, stapling gun, glue, plywood, and carpeting—all materials that are easy to acquire—into fantastic creations. Even though he is now nationally known for his work, George still travels to cat shows throughout the United States and Canada to exhibit his unique designs.

George builds his houses with the help of a designer and an assistant at his shop in Wauconda, Illinois, and has written a book to teach others how to build their own cat condos, biplanes, plantations, or creation in whatever form they choose. The cat shows and book, plus write-ups in newspapers and appearances on radio and television shows, are the best publicity for his work. George will be building his feline fantasies for a long time to come—perhaps until the "leopard changes its spots."

Pet Mail-Order Business

If you decide to start up a mail-order business related to animals, the possibilities are almost unlimited. Besides the usual collars, leashes, toys, and flea products, pet mail-order businesses offer books about almost any animal, pet memorials, natural and gourmet pet foods, dog-food cookbooks, dog houses, animal rubber stamps and note cards, pet tags, animal hood ornaments for your car, and bandanas in various designs for your dog. Cut-crystal pet dishes, cedar-log dog houses, pet doors, and programmable food dispensers are also available by mail.

A mail-order company in Los Angeles specializes in cat furniture and accessories that match the owner's own decor. Often custom-designed, these ensembles are geared to owners who may be a bit fussy about cluttering up their homes with ordinary pet accessories.

Another mail-order firm specializes in pet ramps for cats and dogs who cannot walk well because of injury, old age, surgery, or arthritis. These adjustable ramps can be stored easily when not in use.

Many animal-related subjects are now available on cassette or videotape and can be sent through the mail. Some tapes specialize in training; others, in grooming. One videotape features dogs of all kinds—just dogs! Another videotape demonstrates nature photography, and another shows birds, squirrels, and other wild animals scampering in their natural habitats to amuse the indoor cat in your life. You can even get your cat's horoscope through the mail!

Other possibilities for mail-order products are coffee mugs and T-shirts with animal imprints, personalized checks with animal pictures, dog diapers, and designer pet clothes.

Pet Sitting

A comparatively new industry, pet sitting, is now emerging for pets, due in large part to the fact that most American households have pets. Many of these households have two incomes and no children. When these pet owners must travel for business or work too many long hours, they want their pets to receive good care and attention. Other households with pets consist of elderly or infirm people on whom the pet has a therapeutic effect. And although the owners may not be able to fully take care of the pets, they don't want to give them up, either. The pet-sitting business, therefore, is custom made for these households.

Pet sitting differs from operating a kennel because the sitter actually takes care of the pet in the pet's own home. This arrangement provides security for the pet and convenience for the owner. The pet is also spared any illness that it might pick up at a kennel or shelter.

In addition, many pet sitters provide other services, especially for the owners who are on vacation. These services include watering plants, bringing in the mail, and turning lights on and off, which may deter burglars from breaking in while the owners are away.

Pet sitting can provide you with a flexible career, if you're so inclined. Pet sitting can be an additional service provided by a pet-shop owner, or a full- or part-time career, or just a seasonal occupation. You can run the business out of an existing pet store or from your home. You can have a large staff or run your business as a one-person operation. Since the peak vacation period is usually during the summer, you may decide to confine your services to that time. Or you may want to work year-round, including weekends and holidays. Homemakers, teachers, retired people, or people temporarily out of work may want to put a few hours a week into pet sitting.

Becoming a Pet Sitter

If you plan to start your own pet-sitting business, you should love animals, of course, but there are no real educational or training prerequisites. A business background would be helpful, but common sense combined with a sense of humor can take you a long way. And remember that the term "pet" may include not only cats and dogs, but also hamsters, rabbits, gerbils, turtles, and snakes!

If you run a home-based operation, your initial investment will be minimal. Since you go to the pets' homes, you will only need a telephone (and perhaps a separate business line), an answering machine, basic office supplies, business cards and/or flyers, and liability insurance. If you run your business from a pet store, you need only add on the service to the others that you provide. Grooming and boarding businesses also may add pet sitting to their basic services.

Successful pet sitters might offer you the following advice if you are thinking of starting your own pet-sitting operation: Be sure to get liability insurance and have all employees bonded and insured. You should also have a service contract specifying all the services that the owner wants performed, in addition to the pets' dietary requirements and necessary medicine. You should also obtain from the owner emergency phone numbers, veterinarian's number, list of toys the pet plays with, and required grooming.

Before you sign any contract, however, you should set up a meeting with the pet's owner in the owner's home so that you can meet the pet and get to know its habits and environment. At the same time, you can determine whether the pet is a biter or generally too dangerous or rowdy to take on as a client.

Since each owner has different requirements, the amount of time that you spend with each pet will vary. The pets' personalities will all be different, which is an attractive feature of this career—variety. But if you have steady customers, it is a good idea to send the same sitter to the same customer to establish continuity for the animal.

As an independent contractor, you will be able to set your own rates. The National Association of Pet Sitters recommends from $10 to $30 per day for two visits a day. Your rates may vary according to your location, with higher rates being paid in larger cities. Any additional non-pet-sitting services, such as picking up the owner's dry cleaning, would be charged separately. Most sitters require a down payment of some kind.

If you have your own business with employees, you must train them thoroughly and make sure that they are responsible. Having irresponsible or unreliable employees would be a major drawback in this business—most owners feel that their pet is part of the family and want it treated accordingly.

You will also need to consider advertising your service. Since there are so many pets on every street in the country, there is most likely a need for pet sitting in your location. A large city will need more than one pet sitter. Many veterinarians and pet shop owners will display your flyers or business cards. You can also advertise at cat and dog shows, breeders', and groomers'.

Other Animal-Related Businesses

Financial Management for Animal Welfare

If you are used to dealing with financial matters, you might consider managing investment portfolios for animal welfare organizations, such as humane shelters, which often have certain ethical standards about how their money should be invested. Pet health insurance is also an up-and-coming business to get into. A bank in Massachusetts offers VISA cards to pet owners who also receive an optional pet health insurance package as well as discount coupons for pet food and supplies.

Dog Camp

Due to open soon is a camp for dogs and their owners. It will offer individualized training in obedience and agility for the dogs. Guest lecturers will cover such subjects as agility, breed handling, first aid, therapy, and field work. The owners will have the opportunity to swim, walk, and relax.

Adoption Centers

Some working and racing dogs, such as greyhounds, can be rescued from death by adoption centers after their racing careers have ended. These centers specialize in training these dogs to be pets. The grateful dogs need, in the meantime, only to be boarded and cared for while waiting for adoption.

Pet Theft Prevention

Some business people are concerned with the theft or loss of your pet. Just as your VCR can be stolen and sold for cash, so can your dog or cat. Stolen pets are often sold to laboratories for experimentation. Certain companies help to track down lost or stolen pets by tattooing and registering them. Other entrepreneurs supply concerned pet owners with directories of overnight lodgings that accept pets, so that pets can travel along with their owners.

Pet Muzak

Just as humans are prone to stress and need a feeling of security, so do animals. Just as humans turn to music to calm their jangling nerves, so do animals. And there are cassettes available that provide soothing music at two different frequency ranges simultaneously—one to soothe the owner, one to soothe the pet.

Rent-A-Pet

If you're a single woman who jogs, you may want to rent a dog to accompany you and provide you with security on your runs. These dogs, who have been trained to keep up at your pace, are available at all times of day, every day, and can even be rented by the month. So far this service is available only in some areas, but the idea may catch on. The hotel and bed-and-breakfast industry may offer this service for the increasing number of women who travel alone on business.

"Cruelty-Free" Personal Care Suppliers

There are some entrepreneurial businesses run by animal lovers, such as Anita Roddick's The Body Shop, that specialize in supplying products that are free of all animal ingredients or byproducts, or that were developed by experimentation on animals. Products available through these companies include cosmetics, hair-care products, bubble bath and bath oil, skin-care products, household cleaners, and baby products. Since more and more consumers are choosing not to wear leather, a business can offer nonleather shoes, purses, wallets, and briefcases. Vegetarian cookbooks, T-shirts, and sweatshirts are also available.

Also available through similar organizations are classroom devices that reduce or eliminate the need to dissect frogs or fetal pigs, as has been the practice in biology classes for years. A computer simulation for grade-school students is now available that shows the youngsters which instruments would be used in dissection and how to locate and remove specific organs and magnify them for observation. The program allows for diagrams and animation. Then the students can "reconstruct" the frog and see him as he hops away—all this without a live animal!

Veterinarian colleges can use electronic mannequins of cats and dogs to reduce the number of live animals used for certain training techniques. These dummies have pulses, fur, teeth, and plastic organs. They can be used to help budding veterinarians develop the correct touching techniques for animals of different size and weight. If too much pressure is applied, a light goes on and the student tries again. Films are now available to show symptoms of animal illness and operating and treatment techniques to cut down on the use of real animals in the operating room.

For more information on organizations concerned with the humane treatment of animals, see chapter nine, "Protective Organizations."

Pet Business Supply

Because such pet-oriented businesses need printed contracts and other forms, you could start a business to fill that need. Such a company might offer a wide variety of peripheral materials especially geared to businesses serving pets and their owners.

Green Pet Care

Other entrepreneurs are becoming more aware of potentially harmful ingredients in commercial pet food and flea-control products; thus, a natural pet foods and products industry is emerging. Flea collars and shampoos, combs and herbal powders are now for sale as well as natural remedies for arthritic pets. Other business people supply natural, chemical-free food and treats for your pet.

Pet Transport

A small but growing field is the pet transport business, which usually entails bringing the pet to or from the airport when the pet's plane arrives before the owner's flight. Pet transporters also may provide basic taxi service for pets, taking them to the veterinarian or the groomer. No formal education or training is necessary to be a pet transporter, although this profession does have a professional organization, The Independent Pet and Animal Transportation Association.

The need for such a service exists in most communities, but it may not be large enough to serve as your sole source of income. For that reason, some pet transporters are also either pet-shop owners or kennel operators. To get into the business, you need first a love of animals and second a van or truck. If your business is successful you can expand, hire employees, and send out more vans.

Having boarding facilities can boost your pet transport business, especially with customers who are moving to your city. They may want to send their pet along beforehand and will need someone to both pick up the pet and board it until their arrival. As a pet transporter and boarder, you will need to be on call 24 hours a day, year-round. Your employees will have to be reliable, dependable, and lovers of animals. They must also be good drivers and know their way around your city.

Pet Breeder

You may decide that you would like to have direct contact with only one kind of animal and choose to specialize in breeding German shepherds, or Russian blues, or Scottish folds. This career requires preparation, either by apprenticing under an experienced groomer or by taking college courses in genetics and animal health care. Standards for this career are set by the National Pet Dealers and Breeders Association.

As a breeder, your work will consist of planning matings and exhibiting the animals at shows. You will also feed, groom, and clean the animals and help them through pregnancy, delivery, and raising their young. You should have close contact with a veterinarian, maintain records, and find potential buyers.

Pet Cemetery

Pets get old and die just like humans, and many owners choose to bury them in a cemetery or cremate them. As for other needs, there are businesses that serve pet owners at this time. If pets are buried, they will need a stone or marker. Some pets are buried in caskets, which must be provided. The International Association of Pet Cemeteries is the professional association that sets the standards and regulations for members who are owners of cemeteries and crematoria. Its aim is to upgrade the industry and to assure the pet owner of a safe resting place for their companion animal.

The association provides a seminar, "The Prospective Pet Cemeterian," for those who wish to start up in the business. If members adhere to the basic standards established by the association, their facility will be designated an approved pet cemetery.

Starting a Pet-Related Business

As you can see, in starting a pet-related business, you can fill an already established need by becoming a pet-shop owner or kennel operator, or you can let your imagination run free and build cat condos or sell gourmet pet food and recipes. Since there are so many pets in this country, there are also concerned pet owners who are willing to pay for quality nutrition and care for their faithful companions. Also, pet owners generally like to own animal-related objects such as mugs, note cards, playing cards, T-shirts, and sweatshirts. These all have to be provided by business people. Pet-related ideas for businesses are limited only by the entrepreneur's imagination and the needs of pets and their owners.

Some businesses require little or no formal education or training, but they do require careful observation, on-the-job training, common sense, business acumen, love of animals, courage, and a sense of humor. Those businesses that may require little or no training may be the ones where affiliation with a professional association will be most helpful in getting your business started.

As owners love to talk to other owners about their pets, people in pet-related businesses often know each other and will cooperate with advertising and referrals if you have a good reputation in the field. If no formal training is available in your area, it is always helpful to talk to other people in the business, go to pet shows, work part-time, and volunteer. Apprentice under the best person in the community so that your reputation will be credible.

You may eventually combine businesses, such as those of kennel operator and pet transporter, cat trainer and furniture maker, groomer and pet supplier. Keep up with new trends in technology and medical treatment of animals. Talk to veterinarians about physiological needs of animals or to therapists about psychological needs. Read trade publications, especially the advertisements, to see where you might apply your natural animal-loving instincts. Contact professional associations for membership requirements and standards. They can often supply you with reading lists and educational requirements, as well as providing social networking possibilities.

Is a Pet-Related Business Right for Me?

You should also carefully assess your own personal talents and inclinations. You should ask yourself if you want to work directly with animals, whether you want to own your own business or work for someone else, how much money you want to earn, and how much time and money you want to invest in your career.

You may prefer to work in an office preparing investment portfolios for animal-related organizations. Or your business background may have prepared you for the lucrative mail-order industry, where you can either provide for the needs of the animals or the whimsies of the owners. You may have been deeply affected at one time or another by the prolonged illness and death of a pet and choose to specialize in the design and manufacture of equipment that will relieve pain, suffering, or disability of animals, or you may even decide to open a pet cemetery or crematorium.

Breeding, boarding, pet sitting, grooming, and transporting require working directly with animals. This often strenuous work will require long days and year-round activity. Pet-shop owners and suppliers work more directly with owners but often become quite attached to the pets.

So let's ask some questions that may help you to make up your mind about the type of business that would interest you:

1. Am I more comfortable working in an office with regular hours and a steady income?

2. Does my background and training involve business courses rather than animal-related courses?

3. Do I like to keep records, make appointments, and schedule assignments for employees?

4. Does my talent lie in administrative rather than field work?

5. Do I love to work with animals of any kind, at any time, anywhere?

6. Do I get frustrated trying to explain to an owner what I'm doing and why?

7. Am I prepared to deal with the more unpleasant parts of the job, such as illness and death of an animal?

8. Am I able to do strenuous work with irregular hours?

If you answered "yes" to the first four questions, you are probably better suited to owning a pet shop, running a mail-order business, being a pet supplier, or selling animal-related products. If you answered "yes" to the last four questions, you might be ready for an active career as a groomer, kennel operator, pet sitter, or transporter.

If you can combine people and pet skills, your business possibilities are almost unlimited. You could even become a lecturer or seminar leader in the field you have created. You might become a lobbyist for animal-rights issues or organize pet shows. You may want to work for professional organizations and help set standards. Or you may want to establish an organization for your line of work if one doesn't already exist.

If you have an idea, a talent, a cause, a love for animals, an understanding of the human/animal relationship, a natural curiosity, a need to share, abundant energy and patience, common sense, and a sense of humor, you can have a career in an animal-related business. It's really up to you. The animals—and their owners—are waiting.

CHAPTER SIX

Creative Careers

Some people base their animal-related careers on their creative talents. These people include artists, designers, musicians, photographers, writers, illustrators, and film- and videomakers. Others make it possible for creative people to display their talents, such as book and magazine publishers, museum curators, gallery owners, and professional organizations.

Writing and Publishing Books about Animals

If you open a catalog from any bookseller today or go to any bookstore, you will find a wide variety of books about animals. Some are fictitious; some are based on real-life experiences. Some are about domesticated animals; others are about farm or wild animals. Still others are on training, grooming, and care of animals. Others cover one breed of dog, cat, or horse.

A growing number of books are concerned with animal rights, animal behavior patterns, and animal pathology. Some are geared toward adults, others for children. Some are primarily used as textbooks for veterinary schools. Others are about specific career tracks with animals.

For every book published, there is a writer, editor, artist, designer, and photographer or illustrator. All of these creative people collaborate on books on dog astrology, obedience training or training in police work, naming your animal, jogging with your dog, or showing your pet. Other books take you through the history of a particular animal or breed.

Deciding to Become an Animal Writer

A real writer, it could be said, can write about any topic, but a true love of animals must compel you to write exclusively about them. All writers must have very specific skills which, though rooted in creativity, are generally honed with academic courses such as grammar, spelling, vocabulary building, research, and composition. In addition to these skills, a writer has to be able to tell a story, describe a process, or factually detail a character or situation in words. Writers who work for a trade magazine or newspaper should also possess interviewing skills and the ability to meet deadlines.

If you possess these skills, you need to decide on your career aim, such as whether you want to write books or articles for magazines or newspapers. You may also be interested in writing scripts for films and videotapes about some phase of animal life.

Then you must decide whether you want to write fact or fiction. Fiction writers invent unique animals in unusual circumstances; other writers tell of real animal heroes rescuing people and saving lives. Some nonfiction writers are veterinarians, trainers, breeders, scientists, or animal behaviorists who are experts in their fields and who share their knowledge with the general public. Some writers devote their careers to writing about animals; others do it because of an irresistible angle.

If you decide upon factual writing, your research skills will be very useful, in addition to your powers of observation, curiosity about various topics or subject matter, and ability to organize the results of your research into a coherent presentation. Your purpose will be to inform or educate.

If you decide to specialize in animal fiction, research skills and mastery of grammar are also necessary. But your research may be more for background material to support your soaring imagination and ability to create new characters in the context of a story line. Since the purpose of fiction is more to entertain than to educate, humor, irony, metaphor, descriptions, and emotions, such as fear, sorrow, love, and hate will enhance your narrative. The ability to conjure up animal characters with distinctive characteristics is also essential to the animal fiction writer's craft.

Textbook writers should be experts in the field, but will also need to establish the scope of the book, organize a vast amount of material into a teachable whole, and be thorough and accurate in presentation. Depending on what level of readership the textbook will have, the textbook writer must also use appropriate vocabulary and terminology.

Humane societies, professional organizations, small businesses, corporations, and governmental agencies that deal with animals produce information packets, pamphlets, brochures, and descriptive literature to disseminate information and educate the public. Sometimes these organizations employ a full-time staff of writers, or they may hire free-lance people. The requirements for all writing jobs are essentially the same as far as language skills are concerned—these skills must be highly developed. Knowledge of the subject will often be necessary, which may mean further study, either formally or informally, and a firm grasp of technical vocabulary if necessary.

Writers also may decide they want to specialize in a particular animal or breed, and which aspect, angle, or approach they want to cover. Then they may make a choice between writing for children or adults. If you decide to write animal stories for children, you should be familiar with the needs and psychology of both.

Editing Animal Books

Every writer hopes to have a good editor, one who knows even more about the mechanics of the language, has superb spelling skills, knows and understands the subject matter, has a coherent and organized mind, and does not hesitate to improve the manuscript. For fiction, an editor also needs to be able to feel the emotions evoked by the author and respond to them. Editors have to work well with a variety of people including the author, designer, copy editor, illustrator, proofreader, and word processing operator or typesetter.

Creating Animal Illustrations

Illustrators, artists, and designers are needed for books, encyclopedias, pamphlets, movies, brochures, and medical charts. Some may have to know how to draw the anatomy and physiology of many different animals realistically and accurately. Others may invent stylized versions or whimsical imaginings of animals for works of fiction or animated movies, cartoons, or greeting cards. These may be instructional and educational or purely entertaining pieces. Computer artists create simulations of treatment and operating techniques for animal health care.

Artists may specialize in either domesticated, wild, or farm animals. If they choose to do realistic studies of particular animals or birds, either for books, portraits, or calendars, they need considerable artistic skills in addition to a detailed knowledge of the animal's anatomy, coloring, habitat, proportions, dimensions, and sometimes performance and personality. For example, a wildlife artist may want to capture the exciting physical appearance of an eagle about to descend on its prey, whereas a pet portrait artist may want to find out more about the pet's personality, preferences, and relationship to its owner in order to recreate the animal on canvas.

A Pet Portraitist

Kay Alport is a pet portraitist, specializing in dogs and cats. She has successfully combined her creative talent with her love of animals. She began studying art as a girl and majored in fine arts in college. After that, she was a successful fashion illustrator for major retail stores, both as an employee and as a free-lance illustrator.

Much of the market for fashion illustrators has, however, dissolved in the past few years. Several major retailers closed down during that time and others were bought up by companies with corporate headquarters elsewhere. Even Kay's free-lance work began to disappear.

But creative people can often adapt to adversity by turning their talents in other directions. So Kay, out of some experience in oil painting and her love of dogs, began to explore the possibility of pet portraiture. She feared, though, that nobody would like her work, so she started out by painting a portrait of a favorite dog as a gift for a friend, Jim Morgan, her dog's trainer. Jim liked the painting so much that Kay started painting portraits of certain breeds, although she didn't yet feel secure enough to enter the field of personalized pet portraiture as a career.

But Jim displayed her "generic" paintings and Kay started advertising her craft in national trade publications. She went to pet shows, and Jim kept exhibiting her paintings at his shop.

Then Kay started to advertise in local publications, which was less expensive than advertising nationally, and the customers started coming in. Kay also says that dog owners are easier to find than cat owners because dogs must be taken out for walks. Sometimes these walks turn into networking sessions for Kay and her neighbors.

When potential customers are interested in having their pets portrayed in oil, they send Kay a good photograph of the animal, or more than one if a particular setting or background would depict the pet more naturally. At that time, they specify whether they want a full-face or full-body portrait. Kay has samples of different backgrounds, such as indoor, outdoor, or 19th century, for the owners to choose from.

The customer pays a fifty-percent nonrefundable deposit. Kay says it may take her from two days to two weeks to get the kind of portrait she wants. She then sends a photo of the almost finished portrait to the owner. At that time, the owner can phone or write in any changes to Kay. When all is agreed upon, Kay frames the painting, includes the nail and hook, and ships the painting COD by UPS to clients all over the country. Many of these customers become friends because of Kay's personalized treatment of their beloved companion animal, even though it was just from a photo.

Kay has also developed a line of note cards with pen-and-ink sketches of pets. These come in boxes of 50, 100, or 150 with envelopes. She also arranges for gift certificates to be sent to family or friends on special occasions.

Although Kay was in advertising for years, she says that the most difficult part of her job is self-promotion. She was well accustomed to telling the potential customer how wonderful someone else's products or services were, but it's another story when it comes to saying good things about herself. In most cases, though, her work speaks for itself and her clients are always satisfied. Publicity and promotion are vital parts of an entrepreneur's existence, so brochures, fliers, and business cards have to appeal to the pet owners and have to be displayed in the places where dog and cat owners see them. Kay has a permanent exhibit at Jim Morgan's and a good deal of her publicity comes from satisfied customers. Advertising in local newspapers also brings in business.

Some people, as we know, have more unusual pets, such as rabbits, gerbils, horses, snakes, pythons, and pigs. Some pet portraitists will paint them, too, and not all of them work exclusively with oil. Sometimes a pet portraitist will be commissioned to be the official painter at an exhibition or competition. The possibilities for further opportunities unfold if you keep up on trends, read trade publications, and stay current with upcoming events.

In her studio, which has representations of animals in one form or another all around her easel, Kay enjoys the best part of the job—painting. Kay can envision herself painting cats and dogs for the rest of her life—and looks forward to it!

Wildlife Photographers

Wildlife photographers are in demand for books, videotapes, movies, and television shows. Individual photographs can be exhibited at art galleries and museums or published in books. Pictures of animals, including birds, fish, and reptiles in their natural habitats, are needed to realistically portray behavior patterns, socialization, and foraging. These are usually informative and educational in nature and often relate to the total environment.

Pictures of domesticated animals may be used to illustrate grooming and training techniques, breed characteristics, anatomy, health care, and surgical techniques. Pictures of race horses and horse races are not only attractive but demonstrate winning characteristics. Photos often determine which horse won a close race. Working around horses at horse farms or stables and talking with trainers and owners will give you a feel for the animals and enhance your photos.

Photographers of wild animals also must become familiar with the animals' social habits, behavioral patterns, feeding routines, and care of their young. Knowledge or predator-prey relationships will be helpful in stalking the animal for an action shot.

Some wildlife photographers have branched out from picture-taking to producing videotapes of workshops on nature photography. These videos can be geared for the beginner or the professional and may share tips on exposure, composition, close-ups, and marketing. Other photographers conduct wildlife photography trips to national parks in the United States and photo safaris in Africa and other parts of the world. Some expeditions may be geared toward gathering specific photos for particular publications, such as magazines, trade publications, or books.

Starting Your Creative Animal-Related Career

Whichever of the career paths mentioned you choose to take, you will have to combine both creative and technical skills. It is not enough just to have ideas—you must be able to translate those ideas into a sentence, an image, a photo, or a painting. Each process requires different talents.

Education and Training

Writers, editors, artists, illustrators, and photographers, therefore, have to have formal training in their craft first. Writers and editors must know what makes a good sentence and how to use sentences to form paragraphs; they also need to be skilled in the use of a typewriter or computer. Artists and illustrators must know how to select and use paint brushes, pastels, oils, or watercolors; how to combine colors; how to create perspective; and how to portray animal activities, qualities, and personalities. Or they have to know how to operate a film or video camera; which lens to use; and how to compose the best picture according to light, exposure, and purpose.

Most of these careers require a college degree in English, journalism, or fine arts or at least formal instruction in photography, art, or design. Further education might entail attending workshops and seminars, reading trade publications, networking with others in the field, attending exhibitions, and entering into competitions with other professionals.

Writers should read and write about animals in any context, just to develop writing skills and to learn more about animals. Artists should draw or paint regularly even if they are between assignments, and photographers should always have a roll of film in their cameras—you never know when the perfect shot will occur. If you are multitalented, you may be able to combine writing and photography or illustrating and videotaping. But the necessary technical skills must be learned before any of your creative ideas can move on to paper, canvas, film, or tape.

Employment Outlook

If you decide on any of these creative careers relating to animals, you will have the opportunity to work as an employee on a full-time basis or as an independent contractor. If you are employed full-time, you will receive a steady salary and benefits, including insurance, paid vacations, and sick days. You may even receive a pension plan or tuition reimbursement to further your education.

However, if you choose to work independently, as many creative people do, you run the risk of not having work during certain periods of the year. You will also have to pay for your own insurance and supplies and be responsible for your own advertising, promotion, and publicity. Each choice has decided advantages and disadvantages—you will be the one to make the decision according to your own temperament and financial requirements. If you can exist with little or no income for certain times during the year, but love to work by yourself at your own pace, free-lance work may be for you. If, on the other hand, you like working with other people for a set number of hours a day, being employed by an organization should suit you. Or you may start out with an organization and eventually become independent. For example, you may begin by illustrating books for a publishing company and then branch off on your own, after you have saved up some money and built up a good reputation in your field. By this time, you may even have fostered a clientele who will supply you with work.

Selling Your Work

As a writer, artist, or photographer who decides to work on your own, you will have to generate ideas on your own. These ideas then have to be sold to a book, magazine, or newspaper publisher or to video or film producers for their approval. This may entail some research on your part to see what has been done on the topic you want to cover. Your angle or approach or particular specialty may be just what the publisher or producer is looking for. If you want to submit your idea to a magazine, try to determine if it has recently published an article on that topic. If it has, you may want to submit the idea to another publisher. Or you may want to expand your ideas to make a book-length piece on a particular topic. Then you should check to see which book publishers specialize in your particular field. Local bookstores, libraries, and magazine stands will give you a good idea of what has already been published.

You can also check your local zoo, aquarium, humane society, or animal-rights organization to see if they need writers, photographers, or illustrators for their information kits, press releases and packets, pamphlets, and brochures.

Textbook writers always need writers or illustrators to hire on a full-time or free-lance basis. These books are usually technical and realistic in nature, so you may need to take further courses or seminars in medical terminology or drawing to qualify.

Trade publications for animals include the following:

Dog Fancy

Cat Fancy

Horse and Horseman

Horse Illustrated

Wildlife Art News

Wildlife Conservation

Ducks Unlimited

Outdoor Photographer

Audubon

The Audubon Society, in addition to its magazine, also produces videotapes on birds of the different areas of the United
States. CBS/Fox produces videotapes on dog and cat care. Other
smaller videotape producers are advertised in trade publications.
But if you have an idea for a videotape about animals, there is no
reason why you should not submit your proposal to a producer for
review and possible approval. Videotapes require the combined
work of writers, artists, and illustrators, and sometimes musicians
and composers. For the future, videotapes will probably be as
popular and as plentiful as books.

Some creative people opt to work in natural history museums.
Here they will be responsible for researching and setting up
exhibits relating to specific animals and birds. These exhibits are
largely educational and informative in intent and purpose, but
can be quite creative in execution and appearance.

Still other creative people own or are employed at art galleries
that exhibit the best in regional, national, or international
painters, photographers, or illustrators of animals. These are the
people who can spot talent in someone else, but who prefer to
remain in the background to showcase that talent. As a gallery
owner and/or operator, you would be concerned more with
scheduling and setting up exhibits, transporting, publicizing,
and administration. You will make it possible for other painters
and photographers to make a living with their talents.

And for each business that produces T-shirts, sweatshirts,
coffee mugs, note cards, ashtrays, calendars, bank checks, greeting cards, scarves, belt buckles, watches, clocks, or baby products with animal pictures on them, an artist is needed.

Advertising copy has to be written for these products, and the ads need designers and illustrators. And every zoo, aquarium, humane society, protective agency, animal-rights organization, conservation society, national park or forest, or other organization that deals with any aspect of an animal's life, behavior, or habitat will have exhibits to be designed and pamphlets to be written.

Since there are so many pets in this country, pet-related businesses are booming. With the added emphasis now on protecting the environment and preserving species, much of the focus has turned to wildlife and its preservation. So the market for animal-loving creative people is nearly unlimited. Pet owners never seem to tire of reading about or viewing pictures of their own or others' pets or exemplars of their favorite breeds.

Armed with your creative ability and technical skills, along with a little business savvy, you should be able to combine your talents for a long and happy career. Joining a professional organization and networking with other people in animal-related businesses will help with promoting and publicizing your business. Reading trade publications and attending shows will help you focus on your market and clientele.

You may decide to work full-time for an established publisher, videotape producer, greeting card company, or animal-related organization. Or you may be so creative that you create a brand-new career, never before thought of. If a need is there, you will fill it. The field is truly wide open and new possibilities arise every day for those who are alert, aware, and attentive. Changes in technology and taste, and shifts in society and animals' needs, can put you on the creative edge of a long and happy career.

CHAPTER SEVEN

Careers with Exotic Animals, Aquatic Life, and Birds

*E*veryone has been to the zoo at one time or another and almost everyone has made a return trip with their children or grandchildren. In North America alone, more than 120 million people visit zoological parks every year, which seems to suggest that zoos are very popular places. We all love to see animals that are not part of our daily landscape. We can leisurely watch the big apes or the giraffes or the antelopes for hours and keep coming back for more.

But modern, professionally run zoos have more to do with educating people to the need for wildlife conservation than with entertainment. Much of the natural habitat of exotic animals is being destroyed, and in the process, entire species have become threatened, endangered, or extinct. Sometimes the zoo is the only place where an exotic species still exists.

And that is what a zoo is all about—maintaining animals for conservation. Zoos may house mammals, birds, reptiles, fish, and amphibians. Because of the variety of animals and their many needs, zoos provide abundant opportunities for the person who wants to work in one. Currently there are 11,000 full-time employees in North American zoos.

Working in a Zoo

Although the animals in a zoo may be exotic, the actual work is not always glamorous. You need to be committed to conserving animal species through caring for individual animals to be an effective zoo worker. This kind of commitment requires long days of work, sometimes seven days a week, because the animals need 'round-the-clock care. And what are the rewards? Seeing well-cared-for animals who might otherwise not exist is often reward enough.

Since there are so few professionally operated zoos in North America, the competition for jobs is intense. But the jobs and the duties involved are wide-ranging enough that you might find one that matches your skills and interest.

Zoos require many different people and talents to operate smoothly. Most zoos have people working in the following positions: director, assistant director, curator, scientist, zookeeper, zoologist, gardener, public relations specialist, and clerical worker. Veterinarians, veterinary technicians, personnel specialists, operations managers, and business managers are also often needed. Many of these jobs are strictly administrative or are performed within the confines of the office. Others deal directly with the animals.

Many zoos also publish their own magazines and generate informational brochures, packets, and pamphlets, usually through their education or public-relations departments. Writers, editors, artists, and illustrators are needed to put these together. Guidebooks, maps, and information about specific animals have to be available for visitors. Zoos with gift shops need people with retail experience.

Those who work directly with animals need a college degree, preferably in biology or zoology. Managers often need an advanced degree in animal sciences or business. In addition, you may have to take a written or oral examination to qualify for any zoo job in animal husbandry or administration.

Zoo Director

As director of the zoo, you would function as the chief operating officer responsible for implementing policy and procedures for daily operations, in addition to mapping out any future growth and development needs. You would also serve as spokesperson for the institution. Often the director has an assistant director to help carry out these responsibilities.

Curator

There is often a general curator who is responsible for the whole animal collection. There also may be several other curators responsible for specific departments within the zoo. These positions may include curator of mammals, or birds, or fish; curator of exhibits; curator of education; or curator of research. As curator of mammals, for instance, you would be in charge of just that collection and would supervise all staff who work with mammals.

As the curator of exhibits, you would be responsible for the creation of permanent and special exhibitions. One of the most important functions of any zoo is to educate the public, and those programs are the responsibility of the curator of education. The curator of research manages all research programs and works closely with local colleges and universities.

Veterinarian and Zoologist

Veterinarians and veterinary technicians are also employed at zoos. The veterinarian is responsible for the general health care of the whole animal collection. Veterinarians keep detailed medical records of the animals in their care. Veterinary technicians assist the veterinarian in these responsibilities.

Zoologists oversee the future development of the animal collection. If any permits or licenses are needed to own certain animals, the zoologist obtains them.

Other Support Positions

All zoos need people who supervise and maintain the building and all its physical equipment. These are the operations managers, who usually have a staff of skilled workers under their supervision. Gardeners or horticulturists are responsible for the grounds, especially the animal habitats.

Most zoos have a public relations department that strives to get the good word out to the public about the institution and its purpose. Business managers, necessary for most of today's zoos, are in charge of finances. They pay all the bills, buy necessary equipment, issue paychecks to employees, and make investments. Personnel or human resource departments advertise to fill available positions and interview, screen, and evaluate applicants. A registrar may be employed to keep records on all the animals. Each of these departments also has a staff of clerical workers, including secretaries, word-processing or computer operators, and file clerks.

Zookeeper

All these positions just mentioned are there to support the conservation of the animals and the vital work of the zookeepers. Zookeepers are the people who actually care for the animals on a day-to-day basis. The head zookeeper usually manages a specific department and is responsible for the staff of that department. Some zookeepers specialize in one particular type of animal, such as apes, or they serve as close associates of the veterinarian.

But the basic duty of the zookeeper is the daily care and maintenance of the animals. This means cleaning their living quarters and feeding them the proper diet. Since zoos house exotic animals, much can be learned about them by carefully observing their habits, behavior, and preferences. Behavioral changes, however slight, may mean that something is wrong with the animal. The zookeeper is the one who may spot that change first.

Zookeepers need good communication skills. Because they are the people who work most closely with the animals and often know the most about them, they are called upon to explain the animals' routines, diet, and habits to visitors. Educating the public to the importance of conserving animal species is one of the primary responsibilities of the zoo, and the public relies on the zookeeper to be a general authority on animals.

Many zoo animals are very large and their health care and feeding entails hard, strenuous labor. The zookeeper has to be an educated professional on whom the animals can rely for their well-being and maintenance. Because of the possibility of sustaining injury inflicted by animals, the job can be seen as hazardous.

As with anyone who has to take care of animals, you may have to occasionally count on working weekends and holidays, because the animals' needs cannot be shut off at five P.M. Wages for zookeepers are not always high, so your dedication to the animals' health and maintenance will have to motivate you to do this kind of work.

Even with these so-called disadvantages, zookeeping jobs are difficult to get. As mentioned, the small number of professionally operated zoos in the country and the large number of people applying for the available positions make for a stiff job market. The rewards of zookeeping are compelling enough—maintaining quality care for wild animals, including endangered species— that many people want to do this work.

Becoming a Zookeeper

If you want to become a zookeeper, you will need at least a high-school diploma. Many zoos, however, now prefer applicants with college degrees, especially in biology or zoology. Having biology in your high-school curriculum will be helpful going into any animal work, but especially so for going into zookeeping. Any additional courses in animal science would put you ahead of the competition when it comes to applying for the job.

If you think you might like to work in a zoo, you should consider performing volunteer work during your summer break from school, or on your vacation or weekends if you are presently employed. The more contact you have with animals and the people who work with animals, the easier your decision will be. And there is usually room for reliable, committed, and dedicated volunteer workers at most zoos.

Professional Organizations

Eventually you may want to join a professional organization. The American Association of Zoo Keepers promotes quality animal care and a professional attitude to active members of a dedicated team in the United States and Canada. The association publishes *Animal Keepers' Forum* monthly and provides members with conferences and individual chapters with specific activities. It also makes networking possible for members to exchange their experiences in animal care and treatment and other zoo-related matters.

The American Association of Zoo Veterinarians is a professional group that focuses on those who are involved in captive animal medicine. The American Association of Zoological Parks and Aquariums is the umbrella group for employees of zoos, aquariums, wildlife parks, and oceanariums. So in addition to your education and training, membership in a professional organization is strongly recommended in order to keep up with new ideas, meet other professional people, and share ideas.

Many members find the regularly scheduled meetings and conferences to be a highlight of their educational experience and professional growth. Here animal caretakers gather under one roof, both formally and informally, to discuss and debate specific topics. Here you will find out that no matter how big or small your zoo may be, similar problems and challenges exist everywhere, and that through exchanging information you can discover solutions.

Employment Outlook

All in all, zookeepers and zoo support staff can find many rewards in their work, from preserving endangered species and maintaining a quality life for the animals to educating the public about conservation and maintaining the grounds and gardens. Observing the behavior, habits, and social patterns of an exotic animal and knowing that you are significantly helping to maintain the life of the only member of that species often more than makes up for the long hours and often strenuous work.

The future looks bright for both men and women who choose a career in zoos and wildlife parks. If you are well prepared educationally and have some experience with animals, are willing to continue your professional growth and development, are reliable and cooperative, and above all, have compassion for animals, you have made the correct career choice and should find a great deal of career satisfaction.

Working in an Aquarium

Like zoos, aquariums need both scientifically trained professionals to deal directly with animals and a large support staff to back up their efforts. Aquariums typically have an administrative and clerical staff, educational and research departments, operations managers, veterinarians and veterinary technicians, and aquarists (aquarium keepers) and aquatic biologists.

Administrative and Support Positions

The top administrative person is the director who has overall responsibility for the smooth functioning of the facility. An assistant director may also be on the staff.

Various curators, personnel specialists, public-relations specialists, and various clerical personnel are needed to staff the offices of an aquarium. A business manager and staff would round out the administrative end of the facility and a librarian may also be employed at some aquariums. Researchers may use an aquarium's library for their specialized studies of such topics as predator/prey relationships or population dynamics.

Operations managers and various technical workers, in addition to veterinarians and veterinary technicians who work alongside the aquarists and aquatic biologists, actually perform the daily tasks of maintaining the various species of marine life.

As with zoos, the top administrative positions require a college degree, preferably in an animal science. Experience with aquatic life forms is also necessary, along with excellent communications skills. Public-relations personnel need at least some formal training in writing, and a degree in public relations will help them even further. Personnel managers must be current on all hiring procedures and laws, and the business manager needs proficiency in financial, purchasing, and budgetary skills.

Educational Requirements

Anyone working in the field of animal husbandry should have a college degree, either in biology or zoology, chemistry or physics. A degree is becoming more and more important for career advancement; in addition, it provides you with the knowledge you need for the job.

Some larger aquariums offer classes to elementary and high school students. It is not unusual for a large aquarium to have up to 100,000 school children per year visit the facility for educational programs and to see the realistic habitat exhibits. Some aquariums may even sponsor biology field trips for high school students to the Bahamas. There they will go on snorkeling expeditions to identify and collect specimens to bring back to the aquarium. Sometimes special-interest groups such as the Sierra Club or the Audubon Society will offer ecology camps, field days, and lectures for those who are thinking about getting into aquarium or zoological work.

If you are still in high school, you should take your general education curriculum very seriously, putting an emphasis on English, mathematics, and science. If you are still in college, it's a good idea to start your serious scientific course work by your junior year. You will have to be ready to specialize by the time you reach graduate school. When you select a college or graduate school, be sure to talk to a career counselor or aquarist for the best advice on curriculum or requirements.

Becoming an Aquarist

Although it is preferable to have a college degree in order to become an aquarist, it may be possible under certain circumstances to work your way up through the ranks. If you are presently employed in another field, but think you might like to work in an aquarium, you can always begin by working as a volunteer, just to get a feel for the job. Volunteers can help out in a variety of ways from feeding the fish to teaching basic skills to high school students. The more jobs you tackle as a volunteer, the more information you will have to make your career change. As a college student, you might want to serve as an intern and gain valuable experience while earning college credit.

Another way to enter aquarium work is by way of a hobby. Anybody who owns a tank full of tropical fish will undoubtedly know about the care and feeding of their fish and about filtration, diet, and breeding. Some may even work in pet shops specializing in fish. From there, it's a relatively easy transition to move from the small tanks of the shop to the huge tanks of the aquarium.

People who are currently working as aquarists can continue their formal education by taking night courses to get an undergraduate or graduate degree. Many aquariums offer at least partial tuition reimbursement for these courses. They also continue to learn on the job and by reading trade journals and new books in their field. Membership in professional organizations and attendance at workshops and seminars also is part of their ongoing education.

Employment Outlook

The aquarium, just like the zoo, is now primarily an educational and research facility with a need for highly skilled professionals at every level. Aquariums, like zoos, exist to conserve all manner of aquatic life, to maintain their health and well being, and to educate the public to their needs. The American Association of Zoological Parks and Aquariums is the largest professional organization that sets the standards for those who work in aquariums and oceanariums. Through its work, the status of these workers has been consistently upgraded.

Just as in zoos, aquarium work is often strenuous and the hours may be long. Reliability, dedication, good physical health and strength, and love and compassion for health of the animals in your care are the most important qualities of an aquarium worker.

Salaries awarded by both zoos and aquariums are probably not going to make you rich, but most offer benefits as incentives. Basic salaries are generally higher in larger cities or larger facilities, which would also probably have more room for advancement.

An Aquarium Curator

Allen Feldman is assistant curator of fish at the New Jersey Aquarium in Camden, New Jersey. He had previously worked at the John G. Shedd Aquarium in Chicago, Illinois, as an aquarist and aquatic biologist. He has a master's degree in aquatic biology.

Although Allen always thought he wanted to major in biology, he certainly did not head straight for his goal. In college, he studied without focus for two years, not really getting a good science background. But he did become proficient in English, including writing, which he recommends for any aspiring aquatic biologist or administrator, since writing reports and protocols is part of the job.

In his last two years as an undergraduate, Allen finally took mathematics, physics, biology, and chemistry. After college he spent two-and-a-half years in an immunology laboratory. But that kind of work did not satisfy him, so he took a job with the U.S. Department of Agriculture performing qualitative and quantitative analyses on condiments. By that time, he really knew that he wanted to work with animals in some capacity.

He had also, over the years, become an animal hobbyist, keeping fish tanks at home and watching birds on weekends. He started sending his resume to various zoos and aquariums and got back the usual number of rejections—except from the Shedd Aquarium. His degree, as well as his previous laboratory work, helped him get his first job at an aquarium. He worked for a year and a half as an aquarist before being promoted to aquatic biologist.

As an aquatic biologist he had more authority and was in a better position to become an assistant curator—which is exactly what happened. But before he got the promotion, he coordinated major projects, such as moving fish from tank to tank as they grew and needed more space. He was also responsible for overseeing the total needs of the fish in his care. This work entailed diagnostic work and bacterial study, proper use of antibiotics for diseased animals, estimating compatibility of different fish, and quarantine procedures. Since the tank is where the fish carry on all their activities, from eating to eliminating waste, they are prone to disease both from toxins and from stress.

Allen was also responsible for providing basic nutritional and dietary requirements to every species, for husbandry, and for chemical analysis of the water. Since little is known about the nutritional requirements of some of the more exotic fish, it sometimes became necessary to perform research in this area. Allen was also concerned with any problems with the tanks, filtration system, and pumps.

In many aquariums, both managerial and technical skills are necessary at this position's level, for even though you are supervising other aquarists, you are also probably spending about 90 percent of your time directly with the fish. Only ten percent of your time may actually involve coordinating and scheduling programs and dealing with personnel problems.

One of the major problems aquarists have with their jobs is that they feel they are not regarded with the same respect that other scientists get. Allen and others contend that aquarists are not just tank cleaners, but rather animal behaviorists and conservationists. In the past, there was less respect for the animals, too. Earlier in this century, according to Allen, many aquariums collected randomly and indiscriminately. But today the aquarist and aquatic biologist are becoming more and more professional in their work as collectors and educators. Today's aquarists collect only those animals that are needed to complete their facility's collection or to save an endangered species. They can then breed that species in captivity in order to preserve future generations.

Although the pay for aquarium workers is not high and the workers do not always get the respect they deserve, Allen thinks that there are some distinct advantages to the work. Most aquarists and aquatic biologists really love what they do. They work cooperatively as members of a highly motivated and dedicated team and get real job satisfaction from their work. In a way, they get to be biology students forever, because they never stop learning from their aquatic charges.

Aquarists and aquatic biologists do get to travel throughout the country for meetings and lectures where they exchange ideas and information with others. Allen has also been on some scuba-diving and collecting trips to the Bahamas and Puerto Rico and on a troubleshooting mission to the Dominican Republic.

Allen thinks it is an advantage to work for an employer that has no dress code except shorts and jeans and gym shoes. Aquariums also often have generous vacation and holiday schedules and free medical insurance. And although you may not become a millionaire as an aquarium employee, Allen thinks that you are really rich when you are doing what you love to do. He loves his work, enjoys going to work each day, and hopes to continue in his career for a long time to come.

He also believes that now is a very good time for people to seek work in aquariums because so many new aquariums are opening, because professional organizations are upgrading the status of aquarists and aquatic biologists, and because new knowledge and information is constantly being brought forth to make the work even more challenging. Try it as a volunteer—maybe you'll like it as much as he does.

Working as an Ornithologist

Ornithology, the scientific study of birds, offers many careers that cover a variety of aspects of bird life, such as behavior, ecology, anatomy and physiology, veterinary science, wildlife management, and conservation. As with other animal-related fields, career possibilities are offered in management, field work, teaching, and research. It is a highly competitive field, so education and training will be your key into a career in ornithology.

Education and Training

At the very least, you will need a bachelor's degree to become an ornithologist; to attain the top positions in the field, a Ph.D. is required. Note that course work and emphasis vary between schools. Before you choose which school to attend or which courses to take, confer with a professor or career counselor to ensure that your academic choices are heading you in the right direction.

In college, you should certainly study biology, zoology, mathematics, physical sciences, and biochemistry. You should develop your communications skills, obtaining a knowledge of a foreign language as well as a mastery of spoken and written English. Any research work, writing for publication, and recommendations from your instructors will help you get accepted at a top-quality graduate school.

It is in graduate school where you will begin to specialize in a specific aspect of ornithology or animal science. You will branch out into independent research and perhaps assist in teaching laboratory courses. Your choice of graduate schools is crucial to the development of your career.

An advanced degree in zoology from an institution well known as a center of ornithology, ecology, or wildlife management will put you ahead of the competition when looking for a job. You also want to match your school to your particular interests, such as systematics (the science of classification of living organisms) or biology. Sometimes the best way to find out about a school, besides reading the catalog and talking to counselors, is to actually visit the school and talk to faculty and students. Graduate work may last four to five years for a Ph.D. and most counselors advise that you try to publish articles in scientific journals during that time.

A comprehensive listing of U.S. and Canadian colleges and graduate schools for ornithologists can be found in volume I of *The College Blue Book.* You can probably find it in your public library; it will be a good starting point for your research into the correct choice of school.

As with most jobs that offer direct work with animals, you should gain practical experience with birds before you decide to become an ornithologist. Many budding ornithologists start out as bird watchers. You may want to join a local bird-watching club where you can meet other people with the same interests. Or you may decide to work as a volunteer at a university, national park, wildlife refuge, bird sanctuary, zoo, or museum. As a volunteer, you might be asked to band particular species in the field, gather data, or do research. Any kind of hands-on training you can obtain, in combination with your education, will put you in a very good position for employment.

Job Opportunities for Ornithologists

Since the competition for ornithological jobs is keen, you might consider a related field where jobs are more plentiful. Such fields would include toxicology, wildlife management, paleontology, physiology, and endocrinology. But if you decide that you want to become an ornithologist, and have gone through the rigors of graduate work at a top school where you earned your master's degree or Ph.D. and published articles, there are a number of careers available to you.

Many ornithologists serve as teachers at educational institutions while others work for state or federal agencies. Museums and research organizations also employ professional ornithologists. Some ornithologists work as administrators while others combine teaching and research skills. Just as an aquarist or veterinary technician will not always make a lot of money in their careers, the tradeoffs for you as well as them seem to be a deep sense of job satisfaction and personal fulfillment. Your work may also provide you with flexible hours and sometimes international travel as incentives.

Teaching

Teaching at a college or university is a career choice of many of the more than 2,000 people working in North America in some aspect of ornithology. At the larger universities, research may be a large part of your work. The career track at a university usually begins with the title of assistant professor leading to associate professor and to full professor, usually required of any teacher/researcher. Your base pay may be supplemented by lecturing, consulting, and grants.

In addition to having your Ph.D. in zoology, biology, or ornithology, you will be required to have highly developed communications skills and a generally solid educational background. You will be interviewed extensively and may have to give seminars on your research before being hired as an entry-level instructor.

Museums and Zoos

If you choose museum work, you may specialize in research, become a curator, or engage in field work all over the world. Or you may work in the education department or help put together exhibits and publications. Curators are in charge of the collections, but there are only a few positions as ornithological curator available in this country.

With a master's degree, you may work in the ornithology department of a museum as a collection manager, technician, or preparator. Mastery of the computer is becoming increasingly more important for the creation of databases on the museum's collections.

Zoos also employ ornithologists as curators and keepers, but these positions are rare. Curators at zoos usually need just a bachelor's degree and some previous experience with captive animals.

Federal and State Agencies

Federal and state agencies also employ ornithologists, especially those with some background in ecology. Jobs are available through the U.S. Fish and Wildlife Service, the National Park Service, and the National Forest Service. Most of the jobs offered by the federal government involve wildlife management, conservation, and the preservation of endangered species. State fish and game agencies have recently been developing studies on threatened and endangered species, so professionally trained field ornithologists will be needed for these positions.

The Private Sector

Private-sector organizations also employ ornithologists as administrators, policymakers, and researchers, often to run sanctuaries. These organizations include the National Audubon Society, the Nature Conservancy, and the National Wildlife Federation, which publishes the *Conservation Directory*. This directory is a fund of knowledge for private conservation organizations.

Ornithologist positions in private companies are starting to open up. These jobs may include conducting natural history tours or setting up conservation and environmental policies for the company.

In Canada

If you choose to work as an ornithologist in Canada, your chances for employment are even slimmer than they are in the United States. The reason is simple—Canada has a smaller population and thus fewer jobs. A limited number of teaching jobs are available at universities. Provincial wildlife agencies hire some wildlife managers. Museum jobs are few. Since Canada is a bilingual country, knowledge of both French and English is helpful for any senior position. Otherwise, the qualifications are more or less equivalent to those for similar positions in the U.S.

Seasonal work can be found with the Canadian Wildlife Service, but the number of permanent positions is limited. Private companies also hire few ornithologists, but administrative and fundraising positions are available in environmental consulting firms and similar organizations.

Whichever career path you choose to take, you have to prepare carefully in order to be ready to compete for the limited number of jobs available in education, research, museums, and field work, both here and in Canada. If you are fully qualified, however, and have previous experience with birds, either as a volunteer or amateur bird watcher, your chances for permanent employment with a secure future are assured.

CHAPTER EIGHT

Wildlife Conservation and Management

As we have already learned, both the federal government and individual states administer agencies that deal with wildlife preservation and the conservation of natural resources. Chief among the federal employers in this area is the Department of the Interior and its National Park Service. More limited in their job offerings are the Department of Agriculture, the Department of Commerce, and the National Forest Service. Other federal agencies, such as the Bureau of Land Management, the Bureau of Indian Affairs, and some U.S. military bases, may have a few employment opportunities for those interested in animal work.

The states have fish and wildlife agencies, and there are a growing number of private wildlife protective organizations that target a particular species for preservation and protection. Somewhere among all these choices, you may find a lifetime career.

The Department of the Interior

The Department of the Interior, because it is responsible for almost all public lands and natural resources in the country, is

also the nation's largest federal conservation agency. In its pur-
view are the National Park Service and the U.S. Fish and
Wildlife Service (USFWS). The department is officially commissioned to assure the wisest use of water resources, the preservation of the natural environment, the provision of recreational
facilities and historical monuments, and the proper use of energy
and mineral resources.

U.S. Fish and Wildlife Service

Because the U.S. Fish and Wildlife Service covers the whole
country, including Alaska and Hawaii, it is divided into seven
regions and one research information center. Within the regions are more than 400 wildlife refuges, fish hatcheries, and
various wildlife research centers. As with all federal agencies,
there are rather fixed ways of establishing employment eligibility. The USFWS main headquarters, in Washington,
D.C., will send you a copy of its requirements and the addresses of the regional offices, if you are interested in government work.

Basically, the USFWS is looking for wildlife biologists,
research biologists, fishery biologists, and refuge managers.
All federal government employees are hired at a certain GS
level. The entry-level positions for the USFWS are GS-5 and
GS-7. The Office of Personnel Management (OPM) maintains
a register where you will be able to establish your eligibility
for available positions. The OPM administers federal job
information and testing offices throughout the country where
this register and all appropriate forms are available. If you are
still in school, you should request a detailed description of
educational requirements and course work now so that you
will be fully qualified for federal government work when you
graduate.

Requirements and Qualifications for Employment

In general, a position at the GS-5 level requires that you have at least a bachelor's degree from an accredited college or university. Your major should be in biological science or a related field. In lieu of the degree, you may qualify for GS-5 status if your college education and work experience has provided you with the equivalent knowledge of biological sciences required for a college degree. If you want to calculate your work experience in comparison to college courses, a working ratio is one academic year of college to one calendar year of work experience.

To qualify for the GS-7 level, you need at least a bachelor's degree with either

1. one year's experience as a professional biologist, including any work as a student-trainee;

2. one academic year of graduate study in a biological or closely related science;

3. any combination of the first two that would be equivalent to twelve semester hours of graduate study and six months' experience; or

4. a grade point average of B for all completed courses, or a grade of B+ for all biology courses in your last two undergraduate years, or graduating in the upper third of your class.

The USFWS will accept your application if you are within nine months of completing your requirements, but you must prove that you have completed the required course work before you can actually be hired. You will be eligible at one level for one year from the time of hire, at which time you have to submit a written request to the examining officer. With additional education or experience, you may become eligible to apply for a higher grade. The higher the GS level you qualify for, the higher your salary.

All departments of the federal government are equal opportunity employers, which means that your religion, race, color, national origin, sex, age, handicap, or politics will not be considered as a term of employment.

As you can see, the federal government leaves very little to the imagination for those who wish to apply for a job. So don't expect loopholes, exceptions, or exclusions if you are considering a career as a civil servant. The requirements are quite clearly spelled out and competition for the jobs is fierce. You must learn the many rules of eligibility and comply with them if you expect to get a federal job.

Correspondence courses in conservation, for example, are not acceptable to the USFWS, and most applicants will have to pass a written test to be eligible to be put on the register. Contact your local OPM job information center for information about examinations. Often many more candidates apply for a job than there are jobs available. When this happens, the register is suspended and no new applications are accepted by the OPM.

Positions Available in the USFWS

Once you have fulfilled all the employment requirements and have been hired, what kind of job might you expect to perform? The USFWS offers jobs that are primarily concerned with wildlife management. Generally, the jobs involve managing and studying various aspects of fish and wildlife populations, such as habitat, number, ecology, and health and mortality statistics.

Wildlife and Research Biologist

Wildlife biologists at the USFWS plan wildlife programs, apply research results to sound wildlife management, recreate destroyed habitats, manipulate populations, and try to prevent wildlife diseases.

The job of research biologist consists largely of studying fish and wildlife populations, as well as relationships between plants and animals. Research biologists also investigate the physiology of fish and wildlife, as well as their nutritional needs. They take census counts and study predator/prey relationships.

Fish must be classified and their life story and habits recorded. This work is done by fishery biologists, who also study and apply the best methods for rearing and stocking the fishery.

To qualify as a fishery biologist, you need at least thirty semester hours of college courses in biology, including six hours in aquatic subjects and twelve semester hours in animal sciences. Research biologists must have at least a bachelor's degree with a major in biology, zoology, or biological or aquatic sciences. In addition, they must have 15 semester hours in the physical sciences and mathematics.

If you want to be a wildlife biologist, you will need at least thirty semester hours in biology. That will include nine hours in wildlife subjects, twelve in zoology, and nine in botany. As a general biologist, you will have to major in biological sciences, agriculture, natural resource management, or related subjects as they apply to the specific position applied for.

Outdoor Recreation Planner

You may also qualify for the position of outdoor recreation planner. In order to qualify, you must have knowledge of natural resources and interpretative skills. You will also need the ability to integrate public uses of wildlife refuges and fish hatcheries with conservation. For this job, your communications skills should be highly developed because you will be responsible for various interpretative and educational programs. In order to qualify for the position, you will need at least a bachelor's degree in outdoor recreation planning, landscape architecture, biology, park administration, or natural resource management. Additionally, you must have at least three years' experience in a professional, managerial, or technical capacity relating to outdoor recreation planning, conservation, or similar area. A combination of these would also qualify you. Specific positions may require additional skills in graphic arts, interpretative display, or environmental programming.

Refuge Manager

Managers of wildlife refuges try to protect all species of wildlife and fish, whether they are indigenous or migratory. They also enforce hunting and fishing regulations as they apply to the refuges and other public lands. To qualify as a refuge manager, you will need fifteen semester hours in wildlife courses, twenty-one in zoology, and nine in botany.

Wildlife Agent

There are a limited number of positions available for special wildlife agents, whose job it is to enforce wildlife laws and regulations. To qualify above entry level, you must have experience in both enforcement and investigation regarding all fish and wildlife rules or graduate study in law enforcement, police management, criminal justice, or biology.

Other Positions

Like any large bureaucracy, the USFWS needs administrative, clerical, and creative people to help it function smoothly. Among these are clerks and secretaries, personnel and public relations specialists, budget analysts and accountants, writers, editors, and economists. Biological technicians, maintenance people, and craftspeople are also utilized, as well as fishery and wildlife technicians. These positions are usually classified as GS-2 to GS-5 positions.

Gaining Experience as a Volunteer

The USFWS has a wide variety of opportunities for volunteers. If you want to determine whether you are suited to wildlife or fishery work, you could serve as a volunteer helping with the censusing of wildlife populations. This work would entail banding, trapping, and surveying. Or you could become involved in the care and feeding of animals. If you like to work with people, you may want to work with visitor services. Specialists in computer programming, audiovisual work, or photography are also needed. Each field station has different needs, so you should contact the one nearest you to find out where you could be of help.

Volunteers come in all shapes, sizes, and ages. They include senior citizens and Boy Scout troops. You can volunteer with no particular skills and receive the necessary training when you are accepted. Hours are flexible and sometimes are arranged on a project basis. You will only work the hours that you agree to in advance.

You may work as an individual volunteer or as a member of an organized group, such as a 4-H club. As a volunteer, you will receive an agreement that defines your duties and the number of hours you have agreed on to fulfill them. The agreement can be revised at any time, but it will serve as an official record of your service and could be used to enhance your resume. This will be especially helpful should you decide to make a career of conservation. You can also receive an evaluation of your performance, if you want.

Even though as a volunteer you are not considered a federal employee, you are entitled to some benefits. They include compensation if you are injured in the line of duty. If you were sued for damage to property or personal injury while serving as a volunteer, the federal government would defend you. Also, certain expenses incurred during your volunteer service with the USFWS would be tax deductible. But volunteer service does not count as civil service time.

Wildlife refuges, fish hatcheries, and research stations in all states need volunteers, but the needs in each continually change. You should contact your regional volunteer coordinator to find out whom to contact in your area. Volunteering in the service, as is true for most careers having to do with the care of animals, is an excellent first step in helping you to determine whether you want to work with animals. In this case, it will also help you determine whether or not you want to work for the federal government.

Working for the National Park Service

The Department of the Interior employs a more limited number of people to work with animals in the National Park Service. The service controls 321 units with 77 million acres of land in 49 states. Its primary responsibilities are to conserve natural and cultural resources and to provide recreational areas and educational programs to the public. Within the system are also national preserves, rivers, seashores, and outdoor recreation areas. Among its 101 national monuments are prehistoric ruins, natural reservations, and fossil remains.

Working for the National Park Service are 7,500 full-time employees. Adding seasonal, temporary, and part-time employees, that number can swell to more than 20,000 at peak season during the summer. As with the Fish and Wildlife Service, all positions are filled by the Office of Personnel Management. The headquarters for the service is in Washington, D.C., but there are ten regional offices throughout the country.

Since many park jobs are located away from cities, potential employees must be able to relocate in order to be employed. All positions are highly competitive, so you must be highly qualified to be considered for employment. The National Park Service, like all federal agencies, is an equal opportunity employer.

The service employs interpreters, resource managers, and research scientists for its parks, historic sites, and recreation areas. Some of the larger parks have research centers, and the service also administers resource studies units at several universities.

Within the Park Service, there are limited employment opportunities for wildlife and fish biologists and ornithologists; a few more for research biologists. Usually these positions are above the GS-5 and GS-7 level and require advanced degrees or work experience in specialized fields. Your best bet for employment as a wildlife or fishery biologist is with the USFWS. There are some limited opportunities for fishery biologists at the U.S. Department of Commerce, National Marine Fishery Service.

Working for a State Conservation Agency

If you decide that working for the federal government is not for you, you may want to consider working for a state conservation agency. All fifty states have such agencies and most do similar work. Their names may vary somewhat, but they are usually called the Department of Fish, Wildlife, and Parks; or the Department of Natural Resources; or the Game and Fishing Commission. Most are headquartered in the state capital.

Although job titles and salaries will vary from state to state, the following information will be somewhat typical for all states. For example, the state agency's primary responsibilities will be to preserve fish, plant, and wildlife resources. State agencies are similar to their federal counterparts in that they are equal opportunity employers, that their employees are civil servants, and that they usually have rigidly drawn qualifications and application procedures for the jobs.

Education and Training

Some state agencies recommend that you start thinking about a conservation career by the time you get to high school. One indication that you might be cut out for this work would be your choice of hobbies and leisure activities. If they include birdwatching, fishing, nature photography, or similar activities having to do with nature and animals, you might enjoy working with fish and wildlife.

If you're in high school now, you should take biology, physics, chemistry, and mathematics. Since you will also have to be able to interpret complex and technical information for lay people, a mastery of spoken and written English is essential. Some knowledge of geography and the earth sciences is also helpful.

Since most careers in the natural resource sciences require at least a bachelor's degree, you should carefully consider which college or university you will attend. It is a good idea to talk with your counselor or with members of the faculty or the schools you are considering. Consulting the professional organization affiliated with your specialty is also helpful. Two such organizations are the American Fisheries Society and the Wildlife Society.

In your undergraduate years, you should not try to specialize but rather concentrate on expanding your knowledge in a variety of areas, such as humanities, English composition, literature, mathematics, history, geography, foreign language, and science, including biology, chemistry, zoology, physics, and computer science. High school or college is a good time to get involved in extracurricular activities, such as debating or writing for the school newspaper. These will prepare you for public speaking and report writing.

When you have chosen your major, such as zoology, you should take some more specialized courses in that discipline, such as invertebrate zoology, physiology, or systematics.

If you want to move up the career ladder, you should seriously consider getting a master's degree or Ph.D. You would then specialize in some aspect of your conservation career choice.

The positions that usually require master's degrees and beyond include teaching, research, management, and administration. If you become a teacher, state conservation agencies may call on you as a consultant in your specialized field.

Positions Available in State Conservation Agencies

The field of natural resources conservation and wildlife management needs highly trained professionals who have a broad educational background combined with very specific skills. Typical of some of the job titles for positions within the state agencies are:

Game and Fish Biologist

Wildlife Officer

Game Warden

Wildlife Manager

Game Protector

Wildlife Agent

Fish Manager

Wildlife Biologist

Fishery Biologist

Wildlife Information and Education Specialist

Wildlife Research Biologist

Wildlife Enforcement Officer

Fish and Wildlife Interpreter

Natural Resources Specialist

Wildlife Biologist

Wildlife biologists for the state may be involved in basic research, environmental protection studies, or various field activities such as observing, tagging, and banding birds or wildlife or surveying animal foraging patterns. Wildlife biologists may also collect certain species, work in the laboratory, develop animal habitats, and meet with visitors.

Habitat loss for wild animals is becoming an increasingly common problem because of so much land development and environmental pollution. Preserving habitat in many cases preserves the species, so this work is extremely important for the total environment and is therefore a major part of the work of the wildlife biologist.

To qualify for the position of wildlife biologist with most state agencies, you will need a bachelor of science (B.S.) degree in zoology, botany, wildlife management, or a related subject.

Most states will employ aquatic biologists for their fish hatcheries. These employees will be involved in research, fishery management, and collecting data. They may also survey populations and capture and tag species for analysis in the laboratory. Land and water projects could alter aquatic life and the aquatic biologist may be called on to evaluate the effects of such projects on the life of the fish. Sometimes they will have to write reports on their findings. A B.S. degree or equivalent is necessary for this position, with biology, fishery management, or marine biology as a major.

Interpreter

A fish and wildlife interpreter plans, develops, and coordinates interpretative programs. In doing so, they have to reduce sometimes highly technical information to a level that is understandable to the public. These employees also will be called on to lecture to community groups, civic organizations, and schools. Sometimes they will present slide shows or conduct tours to provide information about fishing, small animals, and other natural resources. In addition to having a B.S. degree in zoology, wildlife or fishery management, or botany, interpreters must have successfully completed courses in natural resource interpretation or communications or equivalent course work.

Fish and Wildlife Assistant

Fish and wildlife assistants may raise fish at fish hatcheries, release game birds, or maintain animal cages. They may take animal censuses or trap, tag, or mark fish or wildlife. For this position, you will need only one year of college with some course work in biology, as well as some work experience at parks, forests, or fisheries.

Fish and Game Warden

Fish and game wardens enforce the rules and regulations of the individual state's fish and game commission. This work usually entails patrolling specific areas and investigating results of environmental pollution and destruction of habitats. Wardens also have to coordinate their activities of collecting and reporting information with other departments. They are often called on to inspect commercial enterprises where fish and game are handled or sold.

Law enforcement on public lands also involves surveying fish and wildlife and teaching classes on hunter safety, trapping, or fishing. Field investigators can yield many arrests per year, especially for water pollution violations that lead to the deaths of wild animals or fish. For this position, only two years of college are generally required, with an emphasis on the study of biology and law enforcement.

Physical Qualifications

In addition to your education and training, some states may have rather strict physical standards as qualifications of employment. Prospective employees are screened for weight; high blood pressure; and vision, hearing, and cardiovascular problems. Your lungs, skin, spine, joints, liver, kidneys, thyroid, and other organs may be checked for disqualifying diseases.

The following physical conditions may serve as disqualifiers in some states:

asthma

bronchitis

convulsions

diabetes mellitis

foot deformities

heart disease

hemophilia

hypertension

chronic laryngitis

chronic nephritis

peptic ulcer

neuromuscular disorders

psychotic disease

alcoholism

allergies

In addition, back pain, colitis, or malignant tumors may serve as disqualifiers for employment. For some jobs, such as enforcement officer, a high moral character must be demonstrated. This usually is signified by having never been convicted of a crime.

Most states will provide you with all the qualifications, salary ranges, job titles and descriptions, educational and training requirements, locations of testing facilities, physical requirements, and any other pertinent information you may need to make your career decisions.

Working Conditions and Benefits

Let's say that you have filled the requirements of a wildlife or fish biologist and have gotten a job with your state natural resources department. What are the benefits, and can you advance in your career? Although your commitment to improve the health and living conditions of animals may give your career satisfaction, you will still need to pay rent and buy food. And in most cases, you can make more money in the private sector than as a civil servant. So there must be something more that motivates people to go into this kind of work.

Some people might point to the progressive career tracks that many agencies offer as motivators. Promotions, for example, may come in the first two years in some states. You will receive regular performance evaluations and career counseling if needed. Your evaluations can be valuable aids in letting you know how you can improve your work. You will, however, probably have to go through a probation period of a few months before you are reviewed. But if your work is satisfactory, you will be in a good position for promotion.

In addition to career advancement possibilities, many states offer a generous benefits package, including health, life, dental, and disability insurance plans; paid sick days, holidays, and vacations; retirement plans; and credit unions.

Advancing to Management

Both areas of conservation—fish and wildlife—have career tracks that lead to management positions. An intermediate stage between biologist and regional manager may be referred to as Senior Biologist or Biologist II, or Wildlife or Fishery Manager. A manager at this level works closely with administrative personnel and is more involved with planning programs and activities or working with other state agencies on matters of fish and wildlife policy. This level, then, has largely to do with strategy, policymaking, planning, and coordination of projects that may have a statewide impact on wildlife. You would formulate methods, submit reports, and evaluate and recommend projects.

You may also be called on to acquire more public land in order to develop more habitats, in which case you will have to set priorities and establish guidelines for the acquisition. This may involve appraisals, determining purchasing requirements, negotiations, and budgetary meetings. It will also require your knowledge of laws and regulations regarding land acquisition and use. Environmental impact studies may have to be generated at this stage of the process.

As reports come to your desk, you will be responsible for analyzing and evaluating them. Therefore, you will have to have a wide-ranging knowledge of ecology, plant/animal/fish dynamics, feeding needs, behavioral patterns, and habitats in order to implement recommendations based on the results of research.

Your communications skills will come in handy at the managerial level because you will be writing technical reports for statewide distribution regarding your plans and programs. You may also write articles for trade journals or for popular consumption. You may speak at community or school events or scientific conferences.

Any work done by state employees requires disclosure to the public. The reports you prepare may be for consumption not only by other scientists or state officials but also by the citizens of the state. You may be required to present these reports orally to groups of constituents. Or you may appear on radio or television shows for informational purposes.

A knowledge of your state's geography will help you plan programs that ensure an improved environment for all forms of life in the area. In some cases you may have to interpret aerial photographs of land areas to determine how those areas might best be utilized. In many cases, you may also have to use computers to compile and analyze field data and store the information in a database.

You will also have to plan and organize large research projects. In the process, you will work out costs and budgeting considerations, allocate funds, and oversee equipment purchases and repairs.

As manager of a staff, you will have to set policy, procedures, and priorities for your employees. If you use outside services, you will have to review contracts and supervise and evaluate their work. You will conduct staff meetings to get information on the progress of all projects under your supervision. You will set deadlines and make assignments for those projects and be sure that the proper methods are employed in carrying them out. You will see to it that your staff has the equipment, funds, and outside help they need.

In most states, you will have to have a master of science (M.S.) degree and knowledge of the ecology and geography of your region or state. Your work affects not only wildlife and fish. In its complexity it may impact a wide range of elements within the community, including business, law enforcement, recreation, geography, real estate, land development, and education.

As fish managers, you may be additionally responsible for setting standards of regulation for the spawning and harvesting of fish, protecting fish populations, and taking part in committee work that oversees these regulations. You may even be involved in making state laws regarding use of fish by ensuring that legislators have the proper background material and that sound fish management principles are incorporated into any proposed statutes. In this aspect of the job, you would testify at public hearings, prepared with essential facts and data.

As you advance in your career from biologist to manager, you will probably be less and less involved in the day-to-day contact with animals. But you can be consoled by the fact that all your planning, strategizing, writing, reporting, testifying, coordinating, developing, and evaluating will serve to improve the environment, habitat, and living conditions of the fish and wildlife in your jurisdiction.

Remember that each state has different educational requirements, job titles and descriptions, salary ranges, and benefits. This overview was intended only to give you a brief idea of the possibilities available to you as a member of a natural resources department. Be sure to contact the specific agency in your state for a more precise, specific, and thorough explanation of their employment procedures.

Some states might recommend that you work on a seasonal or part-time basis as a volunteer before you make up your mind about working with wildlife and fish populations. All states are looking for enthusiastic, dependable, and reliable employees who are also thoroughly trained professionals. Above all, state fish and wildlife workers must be committed to the animals' welfare—and that may mean you.

Working for Private-Sector Wildlife Organizations

If you decide to work for wildlife in the private sector, there are many nonprofit and not-for-profit organizations that work toward the conservation and preservation of threatened, endangered, or tortured animal species. These organizations operate independently of any state or federal agencies and are sometimes at odds with them on matters of basic policy. Some conflicts arise concerning land use that may destroy habitats for many animals; others may have to do with methods of killing aquatic life.

Some of these organizations are international in scope; others, domestic. Some strive for the preservation of whole ecological systems; others, for one particular species. Still others object to the use of certain traps or nets that may inadvertently kill another already threatened species. Some work toward the abolition of poaching or trade in a specific animal product.

People who work for governmental agencies have to follow the land-use policy of the particular administration in power at the time. Since private organizations are independent of governmental dictates as to philosophy and strategy, they are free to pursue their goals as they see them.

Positions Available in the Private Sector

Not-for-profit organizations may not have employment eligibility requirements as strict as those of government agencies, but they do need fully qualified administrative, clerical, and creative people; scientists and lawyers; and personnel and public-relations specialists.

The top administrative titles may vary slightly from organization to organization. Some may combine functions and responsibilities. Such positions may include the president or chief executive officer, who may have assistants or deputies. Generally, there is also a corporate counsel, chief of marketing, business officer, controller, and administrative director.

Chief executive officers oversee all staff and operations. Their deputies work in conjunction with these top administrators and often stand in for them when they are absent. Legal counsel serve as advisers to the staff and often coordinate outside legal help. The marketing directors supervise a staff that develops products and services, advertising, and promotions, in addition to performing market research.

Business managers see to the daily financial and administrative needs of the organization, while the controller supervises the financial staff. Directors of administration are responsible for all operations within the office, such as maintaining space, equipment, and supplies.

Many not-for-profit organizations also employ computer specialists, including managers and analysts, who design and write programs, analyze systems, and produce reports. Benefits and affirmative action plans, organizational policy, staff records, and recruiting are all handled by the personnel or human resources department.

Directors of development supervise a staff of fundraisers and assist local chapters where needed. Developing a steady list of donors, foundations, and corporate contributors is crucial to not-for-profit and nonprofit organizations because they are not funded by public funds or taxes, as are government agencies.

The public-relations department prepares and distributes informational newsletters, magazines, pamphlets, brochures, and direct-mail pieces to the public that will produce a true image of the work of the organization. The activities of these specialists may also include appearances on radio and television shows and at special events or community meetings.

All private organizations depend on membership for support for their cause and for financial stability. The membership staff is responsible for developing services to promote new membership and keep existing members. Research is also vital to these organizations, so there is usually a research group that compiles and analyzes statistics for management, who can then translate the data into reports and recommendations.

There also may be a need for long-range program or planning directors, project directors, and field service representatives, as well as volunteer coordinators. The project director may work on carefully designed ad hoc projects that only last a certain time and have a specific purpose. Field service representatives work as liaisons between the national organizations and the local chapters.

Critical for nonprofit organizations are the government relations director and public policy specialist. Government relations directors represent the organization's interests in its relationships with Congress and other government agencies. They may also be responsible for getting government contracts and grants for the organization. Public policy specialists gather and analyze legislative information and distribute it to the national headquarters or local affiliates. They may also be responsible for working with the government relations staff.

Positions within private-sector organizations, as in state agencies, may vary in title, specific responsibilities, and salary. You will want to contact the organizations individually if you are interested in working for them. Many of these organizations employ field workers, including scientists, biologists, ecologists, and environmental specialists, depending on the specific purpose of the organization. These positions generally require a B.S. degree; for managerial positions, such as refuge manager, an M.S. degree.

Private-Sector Organizations in Operation

Let's now take a look at some of these private organizations to give you an idea of the range of their intent, purpose, and operation.

World Wildlife Fund

One of the older and better known private-sector wildlife organizations is the World Wildlife Fund (WWF). Established in 1961, it claims to be the largest international conservation organization in the world. Headquartered in Washington, D.C., it has affiliates on five continents. And although the panda appears on its logo, it deals with the preservation of all threatened wildlife.

The WWF is concerned with preserving not only species, but whole ecological systems, such as tropical rain forests. These ancient forests, home for half of all wildlife species and many plants and trees from which life-saving medicines are extracted, are threatened by commercial exploitation and environmental pollution. Grasslands, wetlands, and oceans are also being polluted and animals are becoming extinct throughout the world at an alarming rate.

By setting up scientific preservation projects all over the world, many species can be saved through protection of their habitat, acquisition of land, and preserving nature reserves. The WWF's long-range action plans bring together scientists, conservation groups, and other experts; together, they have been able to save or rescue from extinction the Arabian oryx, the peregrine falcon in America, and the Bengal tiger in India.

Defenders of Wildlife

Defenders of Wildlife has been in business since 1947 and is also headquartered in Washington, D.C. This group works primarily from a legislative and educational viewpoint to inform Congress of the need for environmental protection, especially regarding the use of public lands. They work to convince those in power at the Department of Interior to heed their call for less commercial development and more emphasis on preserving wildlands intact.

The Defenders of Wildlife have effectively fought to eliminate the use of strychnine above the ground because it threatened the existence of 15 already endangered species. The organization was also immediately on the scene at the Exxon oil spill in Alaska, analyzing its impact on the environment and reporting it to Congress. They could be considered the private-sector watchdog of the federal agencies.

Sierra Club Legal Defense Fund

The Sierra Club Legal Defense Fund, headquartered in San Francisco, California, likes to consider itself the "law firm" of the environment. As such, they represent not only the major independent conservation organizations, such as the Defenders of Wildlife or Greenpeace, but also the smaller, less famous organizations. For almost twenty years, they have fought to have strict environmental protection laws first passed and then fully enforced. The struggle is often between major corporations or state and federal agencies and the independent environmental organizations.

They have sued the Exxon Corporation on behalf of Alaskan environmental groups to make sure that Exxon will bear its share of the clean-up operation of Prince William Sound as a result of the oil spill of 1989.

This organization will go after any corporation whose operations it feels are destroying the air, land, or water that wildlife need to survive. They pride themselves on halting mining in

Alaska's national parks until they are assured that the environment will be conserved; of saving dolphins, fur seals, and sea birds by working for the prohibition of fishing with drift nets off the coast of Alaska; and on stopping timber sales in the Tongass National Forest.

The Nature Conservancy

The Nature Conservancy has its headquarters in Arlington, Virginia. Its approach to conserving wildlife is to actually buy up lands all over the country in order to set it aside for wildlife, thus preventing its use for shopping centers, industrial parks, or condominiums. The conservancy has been engaged in this effort for 39 years.

A land acquisition begins when the conservancy identifies the environmental value of a certain piece of land—it contains rare prairie grass, or is home to an endangered species, for example. Once the land is acquired, the conservancy manages it for conservation or turns it over to other responsible agencies or educational facilities. So far, they have preserved more than five million acres in the United States and Canada. On these lands are animal sanctuaries, swamps, and wildlife habitats. The Conservancy is an action-oriented organization that works to prevent the destruction of ecosystems and wildlife habitats and to stop the commercial takeover of public land before it happens.

The Environmental Defense Fund

The Environmental Defense Fund, with its main offices in New York City, is primarily concerned with the destruction of marine life due to massive amounts of garbage dumped into the oceans. Particularly harmful to aquatic life are plastic products, including fishing nets, pellets, packing bands, and bags. These plastics may also harm sea birds.

Lawyers and scientists work together with economists to eliminate harmful pesticides, to protect porpoises from tuna fishermen, and to come up with alternatives to dumping plastics into the oceans.

The Wilderness Society

The Wilderness Society has been a conservation group for more than fifty years. During that time, it has concentrated on the enforcement of laws regarding the protection of the forests, including laws regulating clear cutting, road building, and the selling of timber in our public forests, wilderness lands, wildlife refuges, and wilderness reserves.

The society, located in Washington, D.C., has specifically targeted the National Forest Service for its adverse logging policies. According to the society, the Forest Service should be responsible for managing the forests in order to conserve wildlife habitat, preserve watersheds, supply outdoor recreational facilities, and provide timber. The society believes that the Service concentrates too much on selling timber quickly and cheaply, thereby undermining its conservation role.

Whale Adoption Project

The Whale Adoption Project in North Falmouth, Massachusetts, urges people to adopt one of the humpback whales off the coast of Cape Cod. The project is part of the International Wildlife Coalition, which has members in England, Canada, and the United States. The coalition, parent organization to the adoption project, attacks wildlife abuse throughout the world.

The adoption fee for the whale is specifically used in the Coalition's struggle against those countries that are still killing whales, even though the International Whaling Commission has declared a moratorium on whale kills. The adoptive whales are part of ongoing research and investigation by the Cetacean Research Program at the Provincetown Center for Coastal Studies. These researchers are studying behavioral patterns, reproduction, movement, and migratory activities of the whales.

Wildlife Conservation International

Wildlife Conservation International (WCI) is a division of the New York Zoological Society that has taken on the task of saving the African elephant from extinction, largely from the threat of indiscriminate ivory poachers. Together with the World Wildlife Fund, they called for a worldwide ban on the ivory trade; shortly thereafter, President George Bush declared an official boycott on U.S. trade in ivory. Other nations soon followed.

In the past ten years, the African elephant population has declined by half to 600,000. WCI now is engaged in carefully monitoring elephant populations. They are also helping government agencies to acquire new land that will link up already existing parks and reserves, enabling elephants to roam more freely in their natural habitat.

African Wildlife Foundation

An organization similar to Wildlife Conservation International is the African Wildlife Foundation, located in Washington, D.C. This group's major goals are to eliminate the international ivory trade and more effectively and efficiently protect the elephants in African national parks.

Save-the-Dolphins

The Earth Island Institute's Save-the-Dolphins Project is headquartered in San Francisco, California. This project has struggled for five years to stop the killing of dolphins by tuna fishermen's drift nets. The campaign targeted a major tuna packing company. After a major public awareness program, consumer boycotts, and many months of hard work, Save-the-Dolphins obtained from the company a promise not to kill any more dolphins for tuna for any of their products, including pet food.

It all started when an undercover biologist filmed the dolphins drowning in the tuna nets. The project then launched a massive public information program, staged picket lines, sent thousands of mailgrams to tuna companies, and made legal challenges in court and testified before government agencies.

They are still trying to get other tuna companies to comply with the ban on dolphin kills. Their goal is to achieve a total ban by all processing companies.

Outreach Coordinator for Save-the-Dolphins

Sara Meghrouni is the outreach coordinator for the Save-the-Dolphins Project. She thinks that a strong grass-roots organizational background is important for anyone who wants to work for a nonprofit organization involved in either habitat preservation or animal liberation. She thinks that people who were involved in campus activities or student organizations or clubs in school may be best suited to this work, since one gains in these activities the motivation to accept challenges and develop creativity. Working for a nonprofit organization requires an awareness of issues and legislative processes as well as office management skills.

Sara also thinks that you would probably do well to have a business background, preferably with some fundraising experience. Your undergraduate course work should be broadly based and could include law, anthropology, business administration, journalism, and science. Political awareness, involvement in campus activities, and working with other people will be every bit as valuable to you as your course work.

To work for the Institute, you don't need a biology or zoology degree, although these would help if you wanted to work on research projects in the field or write for the institute's publication, the *Earth Island Journal*. If you are thinking of changing your career, you might consider volunteering at a wildlife conservation, environmental protection, or animal rights organization. Your exposure to the issues and the people involved will help you to build up contacts, and your contacts are extremely important in nonprofit work.

Sara worked with animal rights groups and as a canvasser for Greenpeace before she got her job at Earth Island Institute. In addition to acquiring organizational skills in this position, she has also learned how to get the attention of the media, which is quite important in any nonprofit work. Media exposure is crucial in order to get your message across to the public.

Choosing Your Career in Wildlife Conservation and Management

Even if you are not physically working with the animals as a researcher, wildlife or aquatic biologist, or ornithologist, you can gain satisfaction in knowing that you are using your particular organizational, legal, journalistic, or administrative talents to work for the preservation of species, conservation of ecosystems, or restoration of wildlife habitats. You will be able to do that either for a governmental agency or in any one of the many nonprofit organizations dedicated to these purposes.

The choice between the two is fairly clear cut and will be entirely up to you. Government work may provide you with more stability and have more clearly defined requirements for education and eligibility. Since government jobs are funded through taxes, you will not have to be concerned with fundraising. But you will have to follow the policies of the particular administration in power, and those policies may include directives regarding land use, logging, habitat manipulation, and wildlife kills with which you disagree.

Nonprofit organizations are usually governed by a board of directors that will set policy for the group. But these nonprofit organizations are usually focused on a single issue or cluster of closely related issues. Therefore, when you work for an independent organization, you will know exactly which cause you will be working for. Among nonprofit organizations there will probably be less emphasis on educational eligibility and more emphasis on commitment to philosophy and issues.

Whether your job is government or private, field work or administrative, you will be working for the animals whose very existence may be in extreme jeopardy. Your job satisfaction should come from your knowledge that you have made a concrete contribution toward their survival.

CHAPTER NINE

Protective Organizations

*I*n recent years, a growing number of organizations have sprung up in response to the need perceived by many to protect companion, farm, and wild animals from laboratory and classroom dissection, vivisection, factory farms, the slaughterhouse, fur farms, and other forms of inhumane treatment. Although these groups encounter much resistance from those who run the labs, farms, and slaughterhouses, they are finding an increasing number of supporters throughout the country.

The scope of their work is broad and ranges from encouraging the public to buy soaps, detergents, and clothes that are free of animal by-products to providing alternatives to animal research. Or they may point out the danger of certain types of traps and nets or demonstrate how animals actually live on a so-called factory farm.

These organizations may protest possible dangers to performing animals or urge the public to write members of Congress about a pending law that would affect animals. The common thread among their far-ranging efforts is their belief that humane living conditions should be provided to all species and cruelty abolished. They believe that one species should never be protected by the destruction of another. Their aims generally include a deep commitment to the preservation of all species, including humans, through protecting the whole natural environment.

The practical efforts of such groups are generally oriented toward action, with emphasis on educating the public and supporting legislation for the protection of animals. Many organizations focus on protecting a certain species or preventing a certain method of using animals. They launch campaigns that address the use of farm animals, performing animals, laboratory animals, animals in fur farms, race horses, and racing dogs. They may encourage a meatless lifestyle.

Although some groups will occasionally go beyond their own specific interest and recommend actions or collaborate with environmental groups, their focus is what generally distinguishes one group from another. Some organizations, though, are all-encompassing and take on all problems affecting animal welfare as a whole.

Some organizations rely solely on education; others are more oriented toward action. Some organizations were started by medical caretakers, such as veterinarians, doctors, or psychologists; others were begun by a cross-section of people of all social, occupational, and economic backgrounds. All are deeply concerned with the rights of animals.

The Animal Rights Movement

A major thrust for the animal rights movement came about fifteen years ago with the publication of the book *Animal Liberation* by the Australian Peter Singer. Until then, there was little cohesion between those who opposed vivisection (inhumane animal experimentation) and those who opposed the farming system. The book encouraged many groups to focus and dialogue with each other.

To many, the 1970s marked the beginning of an idea—that all animals, including humans, have rights and obligations. The term "animal rights" began to appear in print. And people found out there was no effective legal protection for animals used in medical or corporate laboratories, in farms, movies, or circuses.

The budding environmental movement showed us how whole species were becoming endangered or extinct because of pollution and habitat destruction. Biologists realized that different species have different responses to drugs and therefore couldn't always be reliable for testing drugs meant eventually for humans. Computer technology became refined enough to be used to simulate experiments, and in vitro techniques made research on human tissues viable for detecting diseases.

Prevention versus Cure

These years also produced scientists, doctors, and surgeons who were focusing more on the prevention of disease through clinical and epidemiological research than on surgical or medical cures developed through animal research. In fact, they doubt the efficacy of animal research, noting that after thirty-five years of research on cancer, often with animals, we are no closer than before to a cure. They may further point out that where animal models have yielded little information for the cure of Alzheimer's disease, autopsy studies have shown that aluminum may be a key to its cause.

Clinical and epidemiological research often points to prevention, rather than cure, as the best means of treating disease. Lifestyle and diet are often shown to be the major contributing factors in the cause of some diseases such as cancer, heart attack, and stroke. For example, the three main factors that seem to contribute to heart disease are high cholesterol, smoking, and high blood pressure. Alcohol consumption and pollution probably contribute to a lesser degree. Through effective preventive measures, these factors can be eliminated in our lifestyles, thus enabling us to avoid the more intrusive, more costly—and sometimes less effective—bypasses and transplants.

Epidemiological research has led many scientists to believe that cancer can be prevented through maintaining a low-fat diet, eliminating tobacco, and increasing beta carotene in your diet. Decreasing exposure to the sun many help prevent skin cancer.

Epidemiological studies in the late 1970s also found the unusual symptoms and malignancies of what turned out to be a major epidemic of our time—AIDS. Population studies demonstrated modes of transmission which led to ways of preventing infection.

Later, *in vitro* tests revealed what happens to the blood in human cells and tissues. Actually studying people with AIDS may identify the disease-fighting factors that characterize people who have successfully resisted the strain, without having to inject countless more animals with the disease. If successful, such a study could be a big step toward eliminating the disease.

Animal Research Alternatives

A related movement among medical researchers and scientists has been to replace experimental techniques using animals with animal alternatives producing the same results. For example, researchers who wish to use human, rather than animal, tissue in experiments can go to the National Disease Research Interchange, a nonprofit organization in Philadelphia, Pennsylvania. This group has provided medical researchers with more than 130 different types of human tissue. These tissues, retrieved from autopsies or surgical procedures, have been used to investigate such human diseases as diabetes, cancer, cystic fibrosis, and more than 50 others.

The Ames Test, a nonanimal alternative testing procedure, has helped researchers determine whether certain substances cause genetic damage in salmonella bacteria. A synthetic copy of insulin, which has traditionally been taken from cows and pigs, is now widely available for diabetic patients. This synthetic, called humulin, usually causes fewer allergic reactions than its animal-derived counterpart. In the field of oncology, a new method has been developed that tests potential drugs on the cells of human tumors. The results are then entered into a computer for analysis.

With all these advances in medical technology through non-animal clinical tests, computer simulations, and epidemiological research, it is no wonder that the idea of using animals in the laboratories seemed outmoded and slow when measured against the newer techniques. And it is no wonder that the idea of animal rights in the laboratory grew from an isolated concept to a full-fledged movement by the 1980s.

With the movement's growth came resistance from the corporations, medical schools, research facilities, and pharmaceutical firms the movement was attacking. Using animals in the laboratory and as part of medical training had become ingrained and was difficult to change. Corporations defended themselves bitterly against product safety lawsuits.

With knowledge about the prevention and tracking of disease expanding and coverage in the media increasing, other areas of animal life came under scrutiny. The investigation into the use of animal life progressed to the American farm.

Farming Reform

Many activists date the need for the animal rights movement to the 1960s when people began to see a change in farming methods. Before that, most farms were owned by families who had, in many cases, owned their farms for generations. Chickens, pigs, and cows, even though they were bred for slaughter, were seen roaming the farm land, leading a free and healthy life before being killed. Farmers personally fed the animals, saw to their health, and milked the cows by hand. The animals were allowed to lead a natural social life, and the mothers were allowed to stay with their young for an appropriate time and bear a normal number of young per year.

With the population explosion, however, there was a need to feed more and more people more quickly. Many fast-food franchises and chain supermarkets sprang up, needing cheap beef and chicken to supply daily to millions of people. In order to supply these proliferating franchises with enough meat, the whole farming business changed. Now many animals destined for human consumption are raised on huge factory farms.

In such places, according to animal protection groups, four to five laying hens are crammed into one-foot-square wire cages for their entire lives. Male chicks will be suffocated, drowned, or crushed to death, and females will have their beaks seared off to prevent them from pecking at and eating each other. Veal calves, taken from their mothers at birth, are chained to small pens where they cannot stand up or move and are kept on a synthetic diet that keeps their flesh white. This vitamin-deficient food is usually laced with antibiotics in an often unsuccessful attempt to prevent disease. These antibiotics may, ironically, increase human susceptibility to infectious diseases. None of these farm animals are protected under the Animal Welfare Act, which might assure them of humane treatment during their lifetimes.

Some people claim that modern factory farming, combined with farm subsidy programs, has led to the overproduction of cattle and chickens and even to the destruction of rain forests. Others say that affluent consumers' need for "milk-fed" veal has led to the substandard living conditions of veal calves. Still others blame the emphasis placed on milk consumption in adult humans for the fact that calves are deprived of their own mothers' milk.

About whatever the issue, the protest against factory farms and for more humane treatment of farm animals is growing and getting more publicity in the process. Organizations have formed and ads have been placed in newspapers, magazines, and public transportation systems. These groups actively work against the caged lives of veal calves, breeding sows, and laying hens; and against the health effects of the bovine growth hormone. They also frown upon animal patenting, which would greatly affect farm animals. Some groups encourage a meatless lifestyle, since there is some evidence that the consumption of animal fat leads to heart disease, cancer, and stroke.

Animal Rights Organizations

There are many organizations working hard to introduce and change laws, to educate the public, and to change traditional methods of using and thinking about animals. Needless to say, they will remain controversial and outside the mainstream. But a career with such an organization will never be dull. It will, however, require a deep commitment, a thorough knowledge of the facts regarding the issues, and a great deal of perseverance.

Let's take a look at some of these groups and see whether they offer the kind of work that you would be interested in. Since there are so many, and since they all have different focuses, you may find one that matches your interests exactly.

Physicians Committee for Responsible Medicine

Located in Washington, D.C., the Physicians Committee for Responsible Medicine works for animal welfare in a variety of ways. The group provides education programs in human nutrition and health; encourages the prevention of disease through lifestyle and diet, rather than animal experimentation; and initiates lawsuits, most recently against the National Institutes of Health.

The committee objects strongly to the fact that the Department of Defense does not have to disclose information about animal experiments through the Freedom of Information Act. The committee also notes that military facilities do not have to be inspected by the U.S. Department of Agriculture and that animals used by the military in experiments are not covered by the Animal Welfare Act. They believe that much of the military's animal research is useless and a waste of taxpayers' money.

The committee is in favor of animal alternatives for military use, including the use of gelatin and soap blocks for research in ballistics, current imagery techniques for data on brain injuries, and a computer model called HUMTRN, which supplies an enormous amount of information about any substance ingested by humans that can be identified chemically.

Part of the committee's effort is a compilation of data on military research protocols for the Armed Services Committee and the Government Accounting Office. The committee reviews research protocols for scientific validity, relevance, and humaneness. These protocols must pass rigid standards for control and design.

In addition, the committee sponsors a summer fellowship for medical and veterinary students in order to encourage cooperation between mainstream medicine and animal protection organizations. Students work on a scientific project, which may be published, and attend seminars on nonanimal alternatives and regulations regarding experimentation, among other topics. The program is intended to serve as a forum for discussion between people who use traditional research techniques and those interested in alternatives.

Psychologists for the Ethical Treatment of Animals

Psychologists for the Ethical Treatment of Animals is an independent organization concerned with the suffering of animals in research and educational facilities, in training, on the farm, and in performance. What sets this group apart from others is that it specializes in the work of psychologists and their attitudes toward animals as reflected in their experiments and textbooks. They have developed a scale which measures the invasiveness or severity of research procedures. They also study introductory psychology textbooks with the idea of improving animals' images and promoting greater respect of animals' rights.

These psychologists would also like to make sure that animal use is monitored and regulated and curricula revised to include animal protection issues. As psychologists, they want to study such issues as human-animal bonding, nonaversive training methods, and measurement of pain in animals. Although membership is not confined to psychologists, their thrust is psychological. The organization publishes *Humane Innovations and Alternatives to Animal Experimentation* annually, as well as a bulletin that is free to members. In addition, they maintain a library of animal protection publications.

Humane Farming Association

There are a few independent organizations that specialize in farm animal protection issues. The Humane Farming Association in San Francisco, California, has launched campaigns against factory farming in general and veal calves in particular. The group approaches its work from more than one angle: education of the public, boycotts of the producers, legal action, and legislation. Magazine and television advertisements may prove to be their most effective means of consumer education in this campaign.

Farm Animal Reform Movement

The Farm Animal Reform Movement, based in Bethesda, Maryland, conducts campaigns on a variety of issues, although the veal issue is obviously one of primary importance to them. The movement believes that farm animals, because they are raised for slaughter, have even fewer protections than most animals. Farm animals are caged, deprived, drugged, and manhandled before they are killed.

The movement, founded in 1981, originated because of a growing awareness of intensive animal agriculture, often called agribusiness. The movement operates through a network of local groups and individuals in the United States and Canada.

The group instigated the Veal-Ban Campaign, which was effective in persuading restaurants not to serve veal. It also staged a sit-in at the office of the Secretary of Agriculture and conducted slaughterhouse vigils and a compassion campaign in 1988.

The movement is opposed to immobilizing sows in cages and keeping them continuously pregnant; opposed to keeping laying hens in battery cages where they are debeaked to prevent cannibalism; opposed to resource destruction caused by raising so many animals for food; and opposed to the use of antibiotics in animal feed and the consumption by humans of animal fat.

The movement conducts the annual Great American Meatout, which reaches about twenty million people through a variety of events, and the World Farm Animals Day, which features exhibits, marches, memorials, and civil disobedience.

The organization also has developed a humane farming curriculum for high school students and advanced skills seminars for activists. It is developing a farm animal humane education module for school curricula that will consist of illustrated fact sheets describing the factory farm and offering suggestions to improve it.

Animal Protection Institute of America

The Animal Protection Institute of America in Sacramento, California, also sees a threat to farm animals. This group was started in 1968 and boasts a membership of 150,000 with 10,000 special volunteers. It is concerned with farm animals, as well as wildlife and habitat, legislation affecting animals, and all threats to animal life. It is aware of the factory farm system begun in the 1950s and that the American family farm was not as involved in the intense agricultural business as it is today.

In addition to the plight of veal calves and the continuously pregnant sow, the institute is also concerned with the crush-killing of male chicks and the milking of cows by machine to produce 10 times more milk than normal. Organizations such as this one are also concerned with the effects on human life of chicken that is often contaminated with fecal matter and antibiotics picked up in animal feed.

Animal Legal Defense Fund

The Animal Legal Defense Fund, located in San Rafael, California, was started in 1979 when a group of lawyers decided that they wanted to learn about legislation protecting animals. The animal rights movement was growing, but there was no national organization that provided legal expertise on vital issues regarding their welfare. Today the group functions as the sole nationwide legal organization dedicated to the promotion and defense of animal rights. It defends the rights of wildlife, farm animals, and companion animals in the home, on the farm, in the laboratory, and in the wild.

The fund is trying to give a voice to innocent animal victims of mistreatment, cruelty, or abuse. The group's more than 45,000 members use a network of over 300 lawyers to fight for the welfare of animals in the courts and in Congress. The group created an Animal Bill of Rights to send to the 101st Congress. It will take legal action against any government entities, corporations, educational and research facilities who are in violation of the Animal Welfare Act. It has halted deer and black bear hunts in Illinois and California, for example. Members call themselves "the law firm of the animal rights movement," and they understand that many of the tactics of the civil rights movement can be effective toward establishing laws and enforcement procedures for animals.

Through its newsletter, *The Animals' Advocate*, the fund informs members of pending legislation that affects animals and recommends possible action. These issues may concern animal patenting, wildlife protection, consumer products testing, or genetic manipulation. The fund also operates a Dissection Hotline for biology students who do not want to dissect animals in the classroom. Some schools require dissection as a requirement for graduation, and the hotline has advised students in more than 10,000 calls in the first year of operation. The fund is prepared to give the student advice on negotiating with school officials or teachers, or even to provide legal assistance.

American Fund for Alternatives to Animal Research

The American Fund for Alternatives to Animal Research in New York City tries to bring about cooperation between animal researchers and animal protectors in order to develop animal alternatives in the laboratory, testing facilities, and in the classroom. The fund provides grants to bona fide individuals or groups engaged in research to seek alternatives to animal use. It has been in business since 1977 and has provided funds

1. to develop a replacement for the Draize Eye Test;

2. to teach a special intensive course in tissue culture and *in vitro* toxicology to young students planning biomedical careers;

3. for purchases of a dog dummy (resusci-dog);

4. to develop a poliovaccine test using human neuroblastoma cells; and

5. for a project to assist high school teachers in the introduction of tissue culture into the laboratory.

The fund recently sponsored a program that will supply high school biology teachers with cell cultures provided by the Center for Advanced Training in Cell and Molecular Biology at the Catholic University of America. The center will initiate the protocols and send them to the school where the students will complete and evaluate the work. Complete instructions, as well as videotapes, will also be supplied.

The organization also publishes the results of the research projects it has funded, such as projects on the application of organ culture on the study of neoplasia or alternatives to using animals in cancer research. The organization also promotes the use of electronic animals and animal mannequins in veterinary schools to minimize the use of live animals in the classroom. Videotapes and computer programs are available that explain frog dissection, so that students need not dissect live frogs. (The National Association of Biology Teachers has also recently come out with a statement urging teachers to use alternatives to dissection and vivisection.)

The fund also urges supporters to write to their senators and representatives in Washington, D.C., to urge passage of bills that will protect animals. It also encourages supporters to use animal-friendly (also called cruelty-free) cosmetics, cleaning products, and clothing. (A list of cruelty-free companies and products is available from Beauty Without Cruelty; it includes such products as ultraleather, ultrasuede, washable and leather-look shoes, and canvas shoes.)

Using alternatives to animals in research and products may not provide the immediate solution to animal use, but it may prove to be a logical intermediate step toward eliminating animal-derived products. The American Fund for Alternatives to Animal Research will continue to fund projects that work toward that possibility.

People for the Ethical Treatment of Animals

An animal rights group that defends all animals in all circumstances is People for the Ethical Treatment of Animals, based in Washington, D.C. Their concerns encompass farm animals, fur farm animals, entertainment or performing animals, laboratory animals, racing animals, zoo animals, wild animals, and animal products. PETA's goal is to relieve pain and suffering of all these animals. They launch campaigns to publicize the results of their investigations and research; they stage demonstrations against toy manufacturers, corporations, and government agencies; they call for boycotts of animal-tested products and animals in entertainment; they encourage letter-writing campaigns to Congress on pending legislation; they investigate, publicize, sue, and are sued.

Their magazine, *PETA News,* informs members of their latest campaigns and pending laws, provides meatless recipes and nutritional advice, supplies activities for children, and features pertinent follow-up on ongoing campaigns. The organization also publishes a catalog offering books, videos, and other gift ideas.

National Anti-Vivisection Society

The National Anti-Vivisection Society, headquartered in Chicago, Illinois, has as its main purpose the goal of educating the public to the cruelty of using animals in research or medical testing and training. The group performs its work by holding classes, disseminating literature, lecturing, and forming new anti-vivisection societies where needed. It has a board of directors, which administers all phases of the organization, with the help of a president, executive director, vice-president, secretary, and treasurer.

One of the society's major focuses in recent years has been the campaign waged against the Lethal Dose-50 and the Draize Eye Irritancy Test. Making known the alternatives to animal testing and encouraging the use of cosmetics and cleaning products that do not use animals for experimentation was the chief goal of this campaign.

The society also sponsors lectures by proponents of humane treatment of animals, reports on technological advances and pending legislation that will affect animals, and introduces members to new organizations or to new projects sponsored by existing organizations.

It also produces videotapes that are available from Focus on Animals. Through its membership bulletin, *NAVS,* the society prints pertinent articles, publicizes new books, and encourages letter-writing campaigns against offending corporations or to members of Congress who are on committees concerning animal welfare legislation. The society also publishes a catalog of cruelty-free products for its members.

In Defense of Animals

A similar organization, In Defense of Animals, was started by a veterinarian to protest the LD-50 and Draize tests, animal addiction experiments, and the use of fur and ivory. Headquartered in San Rafael, California, the group claims to have 50,000 members and supporters who are encouraged to boycott specific corporations that still use research animals in their laboratories and to protest against any corporate or educational organization that conducts animal experimentations.

Animal Rights Mobilization

Animal Rights Mobilization has made dog laboratories in medical schools a major target for protest. This organization, located in Williamsport, Virginia, believes that no medical student needs to use live animals for surgical training when there are proven alternatives available. They also believe that using these outmoded methods can not only harm humans and other animals but actually deter progress in finding medical solutions to the treatment of disease.

Association of Veterinarians for Animal Rights

The Association of Veterinarians for Animal Rights in Vacaville, California, was founded by veterinarians who decided to apply their scientific knowledge to the elimination of animal suffering in medical and product research. They are doing this through a national education program that involves television and radio spots and ads in newspapers and magazines. They do not confine membership in the organization to veterinarians.

For the past several years, these veterinarians have also testified whenever possible at public hearings on legislation affecting animal welfare. They are also starting up student chapters at veterinary schools throughout the country and hope to reach all schools with preveterinary programs in the near future.

These veterinarians are also against the releasing of impounded animals for research. They are in favor of using animal alternatives in research, such as computer simulations and tissue culture. In veterinary schools, they favor the use of inanimate objects in order to practice manual dexterity and the use of animal cadavers for advanced procedures. During clinical training, they are encouraged to use actual animal patients only on the most basic operations. They also are against the crate housing of veal calves, and believe that if veal calves must be raised for slaughter, they should at least be housed more humanely and thus enabled to live normal (though abbreviated) lives.

Employment Opportunities in Animal Rights

We have looked at a cross-section of animal protective organizations so that you can make a well-informed career choice. These organizations, all of them either not-for-profit or nonprofit, often operate on limited budgets. Some groups may receive grants or endowments; others may be completely dependent on memberships. You may need to be willing to live very modestly if you are employed by a nonprofit organization.

These animal protection agencies are headquartered throughout the country, so you may have to relocate in order to work for them. Some organizations are headed by and do the work of veterinarians, psychologists, or legal specialists; others are more broadly based occupationally. Most rely on a large group of volunteers. As with many other jobs dealing with animal care and welfare, you may want to volunteer with one of these organizations before actually applying for employment. Volunteering for an organization that has a local chapter or branch in your area would help you to decide whether you want to be employed by that organization before you relocate.

As with any organization, animal rights groups also need administrative and clerical staff; personnel and public relations specialists; accountants, bookkeepers, and auditors; and computer programmers and operators.

Some organizations have a well-established structure, with a board of directors, chief executive officer, and other officers, including vice-presidents, secretaries, and treasurers. Other groups may be more flexible, but administration will always have certain responsibilities, such as setting policy and procedures and hiring and training personnel.

Many other possibilities for employment exist in the field of animal rights. Since more and more laws are pending that affect animals, lawyers will be needed to testify at public hearings, litigate on behalf of animals' rights, and advise animal rights organizations.

The public's growing awareness of the factory farming system will create a need for farm animal behaviorists to work toward more humane treatment of all farm animals, including pigs, cows, veal calves, cattle, and chicks and hens.

Veterinarians will be needed to teach in educational facilities to encourage alternatives to animal use in laboratories and in surgical procedures. Psychologists will be needed to examine and alter public attitudes toward animals. The field of alternatives to animals in research is rapidly growing because of new technologies and the use of human cells and epidemiological studies to investigate the causes of human diseases.

Some animal protection organizations maintain shelters for rescued animals or wildlife preserves. These need wildlife biologists and behaviorists and often wildlife refuge managers.

People with a journalism background are also needed because of their writing ability and knowledge of the media. Most animal rights organizations need people who know how to write press releases and have contacts with the working press to help publicize the organization's work. Investigators and researchers are always needed in animal rights work, in addition to animal advocates in all fields.

For professional occupations, such as physician, veterinarian, psychologist, lawyer, and teacher, you will, of course, need specialized education and training. The same applies to budding biologists, ornithologists, and aquarists.

Many of these organizations have grown from grass-roots movements, and no particular education or training in animal work is necessary for employment. Organizational and communications skills and a deep commitment to the cause are helpful, though, and reliability, dependability, and willingness to work long hours are also valuable qualifications.

As society changes, as technology advances, as new laws are passed or rescinded, new organizations will be founded and new people will be needed for the work. Since these organizations are fairly new in the field of animal work, the prospects for the future are quite good. The work on alternatives to animals, the possibilities for developing products without animal experimentation, the increasing use of human cells for research, and the refusal of many veterinary students to operate on live, healthy animals— all of these mean new employment opportunities for professionals and nonprofessionals alike.

Researchers who are trained in preventive medicine and humane research techniques, instead of such traditional methods as infusing tobacco smoke or cocaine into an animal's body, should be in great demand. The Rutgers University Animal Rights Law Clinic, a new group, will help students in their struggle against dissection and vivisection in veterinary schools. The American Bar Association now has an Animal Protection Committee, which publishes the newsletter *Animal Law Report.*

With the Animal Bill of Rights being sent to Congress, even more possibilities may open up for those of you who work in the legal side of animal work. This bill of rights basically guarantees that animals will remain free of cruel treatment and exploitation, that farm animals are granted basic needs, and that wildlife is entitled to a natural habitat, among other items.

With more and more emphasis being placed on the survival of the total environment through the preservation of whole ecological systems, the plight of animals will be increasingly publicized and more people will be needed than ever before to work toward solving these myriad problems. You might be one of them.

If you are interested in a career with one of these organizations, contact the one you feel suits you best and find out whether your talents and skills could be utilized. Or you may see a need currently unaddressed and decide to found your own group. You need to become aware of what is being done on behalf of animals and what still needs to be accomplished. This may entail a great deal of preliminary reading, becoming a member of an organization that does the work you're interested in, and performing volunteer work for that organization.

APPENDIX

Additional Resources

The following is a selected list of resources that may help you make your decision about a career in animal work.

Chapter One: Exploring the Possibilities

Guy R. Hodge. *Careers: Working with Animals.* Washington, DC: The Humane Society of the United States, 1979.

Barbara Woodhouse. *No Bad Dogs.* New York: Summit Books, 1978.

James Herriot. *All Things Great and Small.* New York: Bantam Books, 1972.

Jack Hanna with John Stravinsky. *Monkeys on the Interstate.* New York: Plume, 1989.

Peter Singer. *Animal Liberation.* New York: Avon, 1975.

"The Scientist in the U.S. Public Health Service." Federal Security Agency, Washington, DC.

"Careers in the United States Department of Interior." Superintendent of Documents, U.S. Government Printing Office, Washington, DC.

"Employment Opportunities in the U.S. Fish and Wildlife Service." Department of Interior, Washington, DC.

"Today's Veterinarian." American Veterinary Medical Association, Schaumburg, IL.

"Your Career in Veterinary Technology." American Veterinary Medical Association, Schaumburg, IL.

Chapter Two: Medical Caretakers

"Careers for Veterinarians." U.S. Department of Agriculture, Animal and Plant Health Inspection Service, Washington, DC.

"Animal Hospital Attendants and Animal Technicians" (Occupational Brief 480), Chronicle Guidance Publications, Inc., Moravia, NY.

"Veterinarians" (Occupational Brief 83), Chronicle Guidance Publications, Inc., Moravia, NY.

"Veterinarian" (Career Brief 1329), Careers, Inc., Largo, FL.

"Veterinarians in Today's Army." Department of the Army, Office of the Surgeon General, Washington, DC.

Patricia Curtis. *Animal Doctors: What It's Like to Be a Veterinarian and How to Become One.* New York: Delacorte Press, 1977.

James Herriot. *All Things Bright and Beautiful.* New York: Bantam Books, 1973.

James Herriot. *All Things Wise and Wonderful.* New York: Bantam Books, 1976.

James Herriot. *The Lord God Made Them All.* New York: Bantam Books, 1981.

Mary Price Lee. *Ms. Veterinarian.* Philadelphia: Westminster Press, 1976.

Carole Wilbourn. *Cats on the Couch.* The Humane Society of New York, 306 East 59th Street, New York, NY.

Dr. Michael W. Fox. "Guide to Cat Behavior and Psychology." The Humane Society of the United States, 1989. (35-mm slides)

American Veterinary Medical Association, 930 North Meacham Road, Schaumburg, IL 60196.

Canadian Veterinary Medical Association, 339 rue Booth Street, Ottawa, Ontario K1R 7K1, Canada.

Chapter Three: Protective Agencies

The Humane Society of the United States, 2100 L Street, N.W., Washington, DC 20037.

U.S. Fish and Wildlife Service, U.S. Department of the Interior, Washington, DC 20240.

The International Wildlife Rehabilitation Council, 4437 Central Place, Suite B-4, Suisun, CA 94585.

The Wildlife Society, 5410 Grosvenor Lane, Bethesda, MD 20814.

The Canadian Federation of Humane Societies, City of Toronto, Department of Public Health, Animal Control Services, 19 River Street, Toronto, Ontario M5A 3P1, Canada.

The Animal Control Academy (A Division of the Humane Society of the United States), 5126-A McFarland Boulevard, East, Tuscaloosa, AL 35405.

"A Wildlife Conservation Career for You," The Wildlife Society.

Protecting the Web, The Anti-Cruelty Society of Chicago, 157 West Grand Avenue, Chicago, IL 60610 (film).

Publications of The Humane Society of the United States:
  "How to Establish Spay/Neuter Programs and Clinics"
  "Responsible Animal Regulation"
  "Introduction to Anti-Cruelty Investigation"
  "National Wildlife Refuge Packet"
  "Plans and Recommendations for Animal Shelters"

Publications of the International Wildlife Rehabilitation Council:
  "IWRC Skills Seminar Packets," Jan White, revised 1990.
  "How to Develop and Organize a Rehabilitation Program," Sally Lewis.
  "IWRC/NWRA Standards Book"

Mae Hickman and Maxine Guys, *Care of the Wild Feathered and Furred.* New York: Michael Kesend Publishing, Ltd., 1973.

Chapter Four: Trainers and Handlers

George Ney with Susan Fadem. *The Educated Cat: How to Teach Your Cat to Do Tricks.* New York: E. P. Dutton, 1987.

The Animal Behavior Society, Department of Psychology, State University of New York, Potsdam, NY 13676.

The Professional (Dog) Handlers' Association, P.O. Box 207, Huntington, NY 11743.

The American Equine Association, Box 658, Newfoundland, NJ 07435

"Animal Trainers," Brief 480, Chronical Guidance Publications, Aurora Street Extension, P.O. Box 1190, Moravia, NY 13118-1190.

Lew Burke. *Lew Burke's Dog Training.* New York: T.F.H. Publications, Inc., Ltd., 1974.

Paul Loeb and Josephine Banks. *The Complete Book of Dog Training.* New York: Pocket Books, 1974.

National Association of Dog Obedience Instructors, 8439 Elphick Road, Sebastopol, CA 95472

Guide Dogs for the Blind, 611 Granite Springs Road, Yorktown Heights, NY 10598

Guide Dog Foundation for the Blind, P.O. Box 1200, San Rafael, CA 94915

The Animal Behavior Society, Department of Psychology, State University of New York, Potsdam, NY 13676

Chapter Five: Animal-Related Businesses

Independent Pet and Animal Transportation Association, P.O. Box 129, Awada, CO 80001

International Association of Pet Cemeteries, P.O. Box 1346, South Bend, IN 46624

National Dog Groomers Association of America, Box 101, Clark, PA 16113

National Pet Dealers and Breeders Association, Route 2, Box 40, Humboldt, NE 63876

Animal Air Transportation Association, Box 441110, Fort Washington, MD 20744

American Boarding Kennels Association, 4575 Galley Road, #400A, Colorado Springs, CO 80915

National Association of Pet Sitters, 1020 Brookstown Avenue, Suite 3, Winston-Salem, NC 27101

Beauty Without Cruelty, 175 West 12th Street, New York, NY 10011

American Fund for Alternatives to Animal Research, 175 West 12th Street, Suite 16G, New York, NY 10011

The Compassionate Consumer, P.O. Box 27, Jericho, NY 11753

Project Safe-Run, 2226 Fairmont Boulevard, Eugene, OR 97403 (companion dog joggers)

Crazy Cat Lady, Box 691920, Los Angeles, CA 90069 (matching cat furniture)

Pet Care With Love, Inc., Box 764 Department MPR, Glenview, IL 60025-0764 (pet ramps)

NASCO, 901 Janesville Avenue, Fort Atkinson, WI 53538 (Resusci-Dog, Resusci-Cat—electronic mannequins)

Scholastic, Inc., 3931 East McCarty Street, P.O. Box 7502, Jefferson City, MO 65102 (computer program for frog dissection)

Patti J. Moran. *Pet Sitting for Profit.* New Beginnings, Department CF, 540 High Bridge Road, Pinnacle, NC 27043

"Personnel Training Tape." New Beginnings, Department CF, 540 High Bridge Road, Pinnacle, NC 27043 (pet sitting)

George Ney with Susan Sherman Faden. *Cat Condominiums and Other Furniture.* New York: E.P. Dutton, 1989.

Groom & Board, 207 South Wabash Avenue, Chicago, IL 60604 (trade magazine)

Chapter Six: Creative Careers

Outdoor Writers Association of America, Inc., 4141 West Bradley Road, Milwaukee, WI 53209

The Dog Writers' Association of America, Inc., Kinney Hill Road, Washington Depot, CT 06794

"Curators" (Occupational Brief 393), Chronicle Guidance Publications, Inc., P.O. Box 271, Moravia, NY 13118

Professional Photographers of America, Inc., 1090 Executive Way, Des Plaines, IL 60018

The Graphic Artists Guild, 11 West 20th Street, New York, NY 10011

American Society of Magazine Photographers, 419 Park Avenue South, New York, NY 10016

Chapter Seven: Careers with Exotic Animals, Aquatic Life, and Birds

American Association of Zoo Keepers, 635 Gage Boulevard, Topeka, KS 66606

American Association of Zoological Parks and Aquariums, Oglebay Park, Wheeling, WV 26003

American Association of Zoo Veterinarians, Philadelphia Zoological Garden, 34th Street and Girard Avenue, Philadelphia, PA 19104

American Ornithologists' Union, National Museum of Natural History, Washington, DC 20560

National Audubon Society, Membership Department, 950 Third Avenue, New York, NY 10022

Long Point Bird Observatory, P.O. Box 160, Port Rowan, Ontario, Canada N0E 1M0

Society of Canadian Ornithologists, 40 National Museum of Natural Science, National Museums of Canada, Ottawa, Ontario, Canada K1A 0N8

National Association of Biology Teachers, 11250 Roger Bacon Drive, Reston, VA 22090

"Zoo and Aquarium Careers." The American Association of Zoological Parks and Aquariums, Oglebay Park, Wheeling, WV 26003

"Careers in Zoo Keeping," Brookfield Zoo Chapter, American Association of Zoo Keepers, Chicago Zoological Society, Brookfield Zoo, Brookfield, IL 60513

"Zoo Jobs," Office of Education-Information, National Zoological Park, Washington, DC 20009

"Zoologist," Careers, Inc., P.O. Box 135, Largo, FL 33540

"Zoologists" (Occupational Brief 237), Chronicle Guidance Publications, Inc., P.O. Box 271, Moravia, NY 13118

"Curators" (Occupational Brief 393), Chronicle Guidance Publications, Inc., P.O. Box 271, Moravia, NY 13118

Career Guide 2000, American Fisheries Society, 5410 Grosvenor Lane, Bethesda, MD 20014

"Careers in Animal Biology," American Society of Zoologists, Box 2739, California Lutheran College, Thousand Oaks, CA 91360

Monkeys on the Interstate. Jack Hanna with John Stravinsky. New York: Plume, 1989.

Don Gold. Zoo. Chicago: Contemporary Books, 1988

John Sedgwick. The Peaceable Kingdom. New York: Fawcett Crest, 1988

The Audubon Society Guide to North American Field Birds. New York: Alfred A. Knopf, 1977

A Guide to Bird Behavior. Donald and Lillian Stokes. Boston: Little, Brown, and Company, 1989

Hiroshi Aramata. Birds of the World. New York: Crown Publishers, Inc., 1989

Chapter Eight: Wildlife Conservation and Management

Department of the Interior: U.S. Fish and Wildlife Service, Washington, DC 20240; National Park Service, Interior Building, Room 2328, P.O. Box 37127, Washington, DC 20012-7127

American Institute of Biological Sciences, 1402 Wilson Boulevard, Arlington, VA 22209

World Wildlife Fund & The Conservation Foundation, Inc., 1250 Twenty-Fourth Street, NW, Washington, DC 20037

Defenders of Wildlife, 1244 19th Street, NW, Washington, DC 20036

Sierra Club, 730 Polk Street, San Francisco, CA 94109

Sierra Club Legal Defense Fund, 2044 Fillmore Street, San Francisco, CA 94115

The Nature Conservancy, 1814 North Lynn Street, Arlington, VA 22209

Environmental Defense Fund, 257 Park Avenue South, New York, NY 10010

The Wilderness Society, 900 Seventeenth Street, NW, Washington, DC 20006

Whale Adoption Project, 634 North Falmouth Highway, P.O. Box 388, Falmouth, MA 02556

African Wildlife Foundation, 1717 Massachusetts Avenue, NW, Washington, DC 20036

Wildlife Conservation International, New York Zoological Society, Bronx, NY 10640

Earth Island Institute, Save-the-Dolphins Project, 300 Broadway, Suite 28, San Francisco, CA 94133-3312

"Careers in Wildlife Conservation," The Wildlife Society, 5410 Grosvenor Lane, Bethesda, MD 20814

"Employment Opportunities in the U.S. Fish and Wildlife Service," Department of the Interior, Washington, DC 20240

"Careers in Ecology," Ecological Society of America, Center for Environmental Studies, Arizona State University, Tempe, AZ 85287

"Careers in Animal Biology," American Society of Zoologists, Box 2739, California Lutheran College, Thousand Oaks, CA 91360

"Careers in the United States Department of the Interior," U.S. Government Printing Office, Washington, DC 20402

"Life Sciences Opportunities in the Federal Government," Announcement 421, Rev. August 1978, U.S. Office of Personnel Management, Washington, DC 20415

Conservation Directory, National Wildlife Federation, 1412 Sixteenth Street, NW, Washington, DC 20036

Chapter Nine: Protective Organizations

In Defense of Animals, 816 West Francisco Boulevard, San Rafael, CA 94901

Animal Legal Defense Fund, 1363 Lincoln Avenue, San Rafael, CA 94901

Association of Veterinarians for Animal Rights, P.O. Box 6269, Vacaville, CA 95696-9269

Physicians Committee for Responsible Medicine, P.O. Box 6322, Washington, DC 20015

Psychologists for the Ethical Treatment of Animals, Kenneth Shapiro, Executive Director, P.O. Box 87, Gloucester, ME 04260

American Fund for Alternatives to Animal Research, 175 West 12th Street, Suite 16G, New York, NY 10011-8275

Farm Animal Reform Movement, 10101 Ashburton Lane, Bethesda, MD 20817

National Anti-Vivisection Society, 53 West Jackson Boulevard, Suite 1550, Chicago, IL 60604

Animal Protection Institute of America, P.O. Box 22505, Sacramento, CA 95822-9986

Beauty Without Cruelty®U.S.A., 175 West 12th Street, New York, NY 10011

The Humane Farming Association, 1550 California Street, Suite #6, San Francisco, CA 94109

National Disease Research Interchange, 2401 Walnut Street, Suite 408, Philadelphia, PA 19103

Animal Rights Mobilization, P.O. Box 1553, Williamsport, PA 17703

Health Care Consumer Network, P.O. Box 6322, Washington, DC 20015

Center for Applied Animal Behavior, 2140 Shattuck Avenue, #2406, Berkeley, CA 94704

Scholastic Software, Scholastic Inc., 2931 East McCarty Street, Jefferson City, MO 65102

"Alternatives to Animal Use in Research, Testing, and Education," U.S. Office of Technology Assessment, OTA-BA-273, U.S. Government Printing Office, Washington, DC 20402

"Beyond the Laboratory Door," Animal Welfare Institute, P.O. Box 3650, Washington, DC 20007

Regan, Tom, Ph.D. *The Case for Animal Rights.* University of California Press, Berkeley and Los Angeles, 1983.

Regan, Tom. *The Struggle for Animal Rights.* International Society for Animal Rights, 421 South State Street, Clarke Summit, PA 18411, 1987.

Singer, Peter. *Animal Liberation.* New York: Random House, 1975.

Stephens, Martin L., Ph.D. *Alternatives to Current Uses of Animals in Research Safety Testing and Education.* Humane Society of the United States, 2100 L Street, Washington, DC 20037

"The Frog Inside-Out," Instructvision, Inc., 3 Regent Street, Livingston, NJ 07039 (videotape)

"Frog Dissection Explained," #B17, Bergwall Video Productions, Inc., P.O. Box 238, Garden City, NY 11530-1238

Center for Advanced Training, 103 McCort Ward Building, The Catholic University of America, Washington, DC 20064

Ingrid Newkirk. *Save the Animals!* New York: Warner Books

"Animal Rights: Why Should It Concern Me?" People for the Ethical Treatment of Animals, P.O. Box 42516, Washington, DC 20015

"Take a Step Toward Compassionate Living," People for the Ethical Treatment of Animals, P.O. Box 42516, Washington, DC 20015-0516

VGM CAREER BOOKS

CAREER DIRECTORIES
Careers Encyclopedia
Dictionary of Occupational
Titles
Occupational Outlook
Handbook

CAREERS FOR
Animal Lovers
Bookworms
Computer Buffs
Crafty People
Culture Lovers
Environmental Types
Film Buffs
Foreign Language
Aficionados
Good Samaritans
Gourmets
History Buffs
Kids at Heart
Nature Lovers
Night Owls
Number Crunchers
Shutterbugs
Sports Nuts
Travel Buffs

CAREERS IN
Accounting; Advertising;
Business; Child Care;
Communications;
Computers; Education;
Engineering; Finance;
Government; Health Care;
High Tech; Journalism; Law;
Marketing; Medicine;
Science; Social &
Rehabilitation Services

CAREER PLANNING
Admissions Guide to
Selective Business Schools
Beginning Entrepreneur
Career Planning &
Development for College
Students & Recent
Graduates
Career Change

Careers Checklists
Cover Letters They Don't
Forget
Executive Job Search
Strategies
Guide to Basic Cover Letter
Writing
Guide to Basic Resume
Writing
Joyce Lain Kennedy's Career
book
Out of Uniform
Slam Dunk Resumes
Successful Interviewing for
College Seniors

CAREER PORTRAITS
Animals
Music
Sports
Teaching

GREAT JOBS FOR
English Majors
Foreign Language Majors
History Majors
Psychology Majors

HOW TO
Approach an Advertising
Agency and Walk Away
with the Job You Want
Bounce Back Quickly After
Losing Your Job
Change Your Career
Choose the Right Career
Find Your New Career Upon
Retirement
Get & Keep Your First Job
Get Hired Today
Get into the Right Law
School
Have a Winning Job Interview
Hit the Ground Running in
Your New Job
Improve Your Study Skills
Jump Start a Stalled Career
Land a Better Job

Launch Your Career in TV
News
Make the Right Career Moves
Market Your College Degree
Move from College into a
Secure Job
Negotiate the Raise You
Deserve
Prepare a *Curriculum Vitae*
Prepare for College
Run Your Own Home
Business
Succeed in College
Succeed in High School
Write a Winning Resume
Write Successful Cover
Letters
Write Term Papers & Reports
Write Your College
Application Essay

OPPORTUNITIES IN
This extensive series provides
detailed information on
nearly 150 individual career
fields.

RESUMES FOR
Advertising Careers
Banking and Financial
Careers
Business Management
Careers
College Students &
Recent Graduates
Communications Careers
Education Careers
Engineering Careers
Environmental Careers
Health and Medical Careers
High School Graduates
High Tech Careers
Midcareer Job Changes
Sales and Marketing Careers
Scientific and Technical
Careers
Social Service Careers
The First-Time Job Hunter

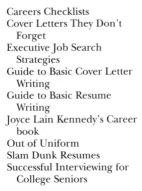

VGM Career Horizons
a division of NTC *Publishing Group*
4255 West Touhy Avenue
Lincolnwood, Illinois 60646–1975